23 Palazzo Pitti	30 University of Florence	37 Palazzo Davanzati
24 Forte Belvedere	31 Hospital of San Giovanni di Dio	38 Palazzo Rucellai
25 Bardini Museum	32 Church of S. Firenze	39 Church of San Gaetano
26 Church of San Miniato	33 Convent of the Badia	40 Church of San Frediano
27 Church of Santa Croce	34 Arte della Lana	41 Sinagoga
28 Dante's House	35 Palazzo Spini Feroni	42 Palazzo della Gherardesca
29 Palazzo di Parte Guelfa	36 Palazzo Corsini	43 Stadio Communale

Florence
Ordeal by Water

INTRODUCED BY
Vanessa Nicolson

Florence
Ordeal by Water

Kathrine Kressmann Taylor

MANDERLEY PRESS

Named for the house in Daphne du Maurier's novel *Rebecca*, Manderley Press finds forgotten or out-of-print books that were deeply inspired by a building, city or landmark, and brings those lost publications back to life for a contemporary audience.

We love selling our titles through bookshops around the world, and we especially delight in posting them to customers from our offices here in London. Buying from us direct makes a huge difference in supporting our independent press, allowing us to reinvest in future titles and exciting commissions. As a thank you, we include matching bookmarks created exclusively for manderleypress.com readers.

The books all feature a specially commissioned introduction and cover, with both the author and the artist chosen for their connections to the places at the heart of each title. Cover artwork is also available to purchase, as signed giclée art prints.

Every Manderley Press title is exquisitely produced as a small hardback edition, printed on luxurious paper in the UK, and quarter-bound in real cloth with head and tail bands too.

For more information and a full list of published titles, please visit www.manderleypress.com.

This hardback edition published in 2024 by Manderley Press
www.manderleypress.com

First published in 1967 by Hamish Hamilton Ltd

Copyright © Kathrine Kressmann Taylor 1967
Introduction © Vanessa Nicolson 2024
Cover and illustrations © Agnesbic 2024

The right of Kathrine Kressmann Taylor to be identified as Author of this work has been asserted by her in accordance with the Copyright, Designs and Patents Act 1988.

All rights reserved. No part of this publication may be reproduced, stored in or introduced into a retrieval system, or transmitted, in any form, or by any means (electronic, mechanical, photocopying, recording or otherwise) without the prior written permission of the publisher.

ISBN: 978-1-9196421-8-5

Typeset in Chiswick and Chiswick Sans by Commercial Type
Designed by Myfanwy Vernon-Hunt, This-Side
Printed and bound by Gomer Press

CONTENTS

Introduction
Vanessa Nicolson
9

CHAPTER ONE
La Piena
16

CHAPTER TWO
Desolazione
48

CHAPTER THREE
Fango
84

CHAPTER FOUR
Soccorsi a Firenze
103

CHAPTER FIVE
Si Ricomincia
119

CHAPTER SIX
Natale
147

CHAPTER SEVEN
Speriamo
156

INTRODUCTION

Vanessa Nicolson

In recent years the characterful *pensione*, of the type described by E.M. Forster in his novel *Room with a View*, has more or less disappeared, overtaken by hotels and apartment rentals, but when Kathrine Kressmann Taylor arrived in Florence in 1966, there was a profusion of these small, homely boarding houses on offer. As a child in growing up in the 1960s with my Italian mother and grandparents, I lived below a typical one. The *pensione Annalena* catered to paying guests who had chosen to spend a few months – sometimes years – in Florence, attracted to its cultural treasures and cheap way of life. My mother and grandmother refused to cook, so we took our meals in the dining room of the *pensione*, where we would be served some form of pasta or soup, followed by meat or fish, and rounded off with a piece of fruit. Irma the waitress and her younger brother Guliano were for me part of the fabric of the place, as were the other diners I observed and who occasionally became my friends: typically an English family with a girl my age enjoying a summer holiday; a married couple of

American academics on sabbatical; a retired woman perusing her guidebook over dinner.

Kathrine Kressmann Taylor might have been such a guest. The Florentine *pensione* she came to after twenty-five years teaching at the University of Gettysburg, Pennsylvania, was, like the one of my childhood, on the top floor of an old palazzo, staffed by loyal retainers who worked there for years and were completely invested in the place. Instead of Irma and Giuliano, we have Aldo and Alberto, with the resident guests moulded from a similar cast of archetypes: the Professor, the Contessa, the retired Consul-General and his wife, and a 'lanky young man in his twenties' who proves energetic and helpful. When things go awry, Dario (the Cook) valiantly attempts to maintain standards by continuing to produce *pollo cacciatore* and other delicacies for his guests.

And things do go horribly awry.

In 1966 Kathrine was on the cusp of changing her life. Born in Portland, Oregon, she had worked as an advertising copywriter in the 1920s and married Elliott Taylor, who owned an advertising agency. The couple moved from San Francisco to New York, where Kressmann found success with an epistolary novella *Address Unknown,* published first in *Story* magazine, then reprinted in book form in 1939. The fictional account of a friendship torn apart by the rise of Nazism found a receptive readership and became an instant success, made into a film by Columbia Pictures in 1944, and later adapted for the stage. Similar themes were explored in her next book, *Until That Day,* published in 1942. From then on she taught humanities, journalism and creative writing until on retirement, and a widow for over a decade, she decided to make the move to Florence. She was sixty-three years old.

Her *Florence: Ordeal by Water* is written in diary form as events unfold (in fact it was also published under the title *Diary of Florence in Flood*). It opens on November 3, 1966, the eve of the annual national holiday that for Italy commemorates the end of the First World War. It had been raining relentlessly throughout the month of October, and we see the author battling through the windy downpour, jumping onto a crowded bus to reach, drenched – or *'tutta bagnata'* as she uses the Italian phrase – the huge wooden outer doors of the *pensione* that overlooks the Arno river.

To get there we walk alongside her on a map of landmarks; *Via Porta Santa Maria* near the famous *Ponte Vecchio*, and then on towards the bridge named after the Florentine explorer *Amerigo Vespucci*, past the elegant palace fronts of the *Lungarno*, the 'embankment' that runs alongside the river Arno. The place names will be familiar to those who know Florence, and this habit of peppering precise locations with Italian comments expressed by citizens the author encounters over the following weeks, imbues a genuine sense of immediacy and spirit of place throughout the book.

The headings of the seven chapters are also presented in Italian, and give shape to the account, providing a sort of narrative arc that leads from *Desolazione* to *Si Ricomincia* and, finally, *Speriamo*. 'We start again' and 'Let's Hope' are phrases repeated in various ways by bewildered citizens battered by the events that unfolded on the night of 3rd–4th November. In the first chapter *La Piena* – referring to the Flood but literally translated as the 'Full One' – the Arno is the dominant character. Kressmann opens her bedroom shutters and faces not the usual picturesque view but a 'tumultuous mass of water ... a snarling brown torrent of terrific velocity, spiralling in whirlpools and counter currents'. The river as evil predator, a threatening, engulfing power, bursting its banks and taking along with it uprooted trees, oil drums, window shutters, and all sorts of other detritus along with it.

Within this kidnapped debris Kressmann observes a child's red ball, and 'a chair sailing serenely, its arms and carved back above the water and holding steady and upright as if inviting someone to take a seat'. Later on, she notes with sadness the stock belonging to the artisans and shop keepers that is reduced to unsaleable rubbish: the 'sopping furs' hanging outside the *pelliceria* 'like poor drowned cats', the goldsmiths on their knees in the mud, scavenging by candlelight in the hope of saving some of their precious merchandise. The images are cinematic, underpinned by psychological insights – her imagery brings poetry to reportage, and highlights the damage not only to the vast cultural heritage of Florence, but to the livelihood and well-being of its inhabitants. And not only the human inhabitants: the rescue mission to release the poor swan imprisoned by oil and mud could be a short story in itself.

Throughout, Kressmann acknowledges the pride Florentines feel for their city's artistic achievements, and she feels it herself. From the domed Cathedral, through the art of the Renaissance and beyond, there is a concentration of works of art made by highly skilled artists and artisans, both well-known and anonymous. The historic centre does not cover a very large area, but at every corner there was a notable building or work of art affected by the force of the Flood. Churches suffered the loss of priceless frescoes and paintings that had managed to survive for hundreds of years, and even previous floods. Rare manuscripts and innumerable volumes were ruined in the National Library; public monuments were battered and covered with malodorous *'nafta'*, the dark, muddy oil that stained everything it touched.

As a journalist picking her way through streets choked with mud and debris, Kressmann details the damage: the gaping holes where Ghiberti's relief panels – part of the doors named 'Doors of Paradise' by Michelangelo – were ripped off by the force of the flooding water; the oil lines on the walls and doors of Santa Croce; the fears for the heritage that may be beyond restoration. And she wonders how the Florentines, 'whose treasures these are' will be able to stand it.

But then the *Angeli del Fango* appear, the volunteers who turned up from all over Italy, then from further afield. Named 'Mud Angels' because of their mud-splattered appearance, these young people arrived in vast numbers to help with the clearing up and restoration. There is salvation, and Kressmann's diary gathers a momentum of hope. Streets are being cleared, services are back on, works of art and the infrastructure of people's lives are being put back together. Cultural life is getting back on track. An opera is on at the *Teatro Comunale*, the shops are re-opening, museums can be visited, the Via Tornabuoni is resplendent with Christmas decorations. There is still some anxiety about the future, but the world has taken Florence to its heart. Financial help rolls in to repair hospitals and schools, warm clothing for the dispossessed is distributed, committees and conferences are organised to discuss the best way forward, art historians, restorers and conservators arrive to offer their expertise.

The shopkeepers, however, are still anxious. When Kressmann goes into a shop she is asked nervously, 'Will they come back? Do you think the tourists will come back?'

They need not have worried. Walk around Florence today, and the world swarms around you. But the hoards of tourists that now crowd the streets are generally unaware of the little plaques high above their heads that mark where the flood water reached. Kressmann's diary is important because it offers a snapshot of that history in the making, a story of damage and destruction, but also one of recovery, resilience and regeneration.

Vanessa Nicolson, 2004

Acknowledgement

For their generosity in helping me to obtain an accurate and intimate picture of the state of Florence in February, and for special courtesies, my grateful acknowledgements are due to Miss Esther Sperry, Signora Betti Gambaccini, Miss Deborah Atkinson, Professor Curtis Shell of CRIA, Mr Harold Horan, American Consul at Florence, Signor Franco Nencini of the *Nazione*, the Honourable Piero Bargellini, Sindaco of Florence, and a Florentine gentlewoman who does not wish her name to appear.

Kathrine K. Taylor

Al popolo Fiorentino in onore

CHAPTER ONE

La Piena

November 3, 1966

The festa celebrating Italian victory in the First World War falls on November 4, and in Florence the raincoated crowds pouring homeward through the narrow streets in the centre of town at six on the evening of the third look cheerful in spite of the downpour. *Domani è festa*, the shops will be closed, there will be a holiday from work, the second festa in a pleasant week.

This is, however, a torrential rain. October was a wet month all through Northern Italy, and after two bright days November has settled down to outdo October with a new drenching. Women protected by umbrellas and overshoes shrink into doorways to wait for a respite in the driving rain that will soak them to the knees within fifty feet, but there is no letup. Buses pass, crammed to the doors, all the taxis filled already. Impatient young men cover their heads with copies of the *Nazione Sera*, wrap their overcoats tightly around them, and set off through the deluge.

Sloshing homeward, my umbrella twisting under the wet wind (I have just been for a fitting of a winter skirt in Via Porta Santa Maria near the Ponte Vecchio), I catch a jammed bus for a few blocks to the Ponte Amerigo Vespucci and then hug the palace fronts along the Lungarno, to arrive, *tutta bagnata*, at the huge wooden outer doors of the *pensione* on the Arno. It is a night to stay indoors, despite a concert in the Hall of the Five Hundred, a night for a hot bath and a cognac, bed and a good book, with the sound of the rain drumming on the shutters a comfortable soporific.

Friday, November 4

Dawn comes at six with a faint gleam of grey through the slats of the shutters (all Italian houses are sealed tight during the night), but a flick of the switch of the bedside lamp brings no responsive glow of light. A cigarette lighter shows the hour. I stumble out of bed and grope my way to the wall switch, which proves dead too, and then feel my way through the gloom to the windows and push the shutters back into their recesses. My first impression is that it is darkly overcast and still raining hard; then I stand gaping at the river.

The Arno? That peaceful green stream winds slowly between high embankments, the one on this side of concrete topped by a stout four-foot brick and concrete wall, and below the walls the river is bordered by grassy tree-covered flatlands, where fishermen line the banks on holiday mornings, the men in waders venturing out nearly to midstream with their lines.

The Arno had risen and spread during the October rains and become a true river, broad and smooth, perhaps three feet higher than ordinary. But this river!

A tumultuous mass of water stretches from bank to bank, perhaps four feet below the tops of the twenty-five-foot walls, a snarling brown torrent of terrific velocity, spiralling in whirlpools and countercurrents that send waves running backward; and its colour is a rich brown, a boiling *caffé-latte* brown streaked with crests the colour of dirty cream.

This tremendous water carries mats of debris: straw, twigs, leafy branches, rags, a litter that the river sucks down and spews up again in a swelling turbulence. Its thunderous rush holds me tense at the window, as any movement of great force can lay a spell on the eyes. All I can think of is that it is as magnificent as it is threatening, a river in spate moving at full stress, its surface twisting with curling ropes of water that smack together and go up in spouts of foam. The flood is absolute as a forest fire is absolute or a full gale stripping the countryside and bending down all the trees.

Here down the torrent comes a tree, uprooted, the tangled root structure washed clean by the water, the branches trailing thick leaves. A red oil drum comes bobbing high; then two more trees slide by, their roots a floating snarl – and how big they are! There must have been terrible cloudbursts up in the hills of the Casentino when we had that drenching rain last night – this same drenching rain, for it is still coming down in *scrosci*. There are electric lights visible in two buildings across the Arno, but these go out while I am watching, while the dawn light is still closer to darkness than today.

I mark a measuring point on the opposite side, a hole in the brick front of the rock-crushing plant, whose flat-bottomed barges are leaping and clashing together at their moorings, and after a few minutes' watch I conclude that the river is still rising. It can't be far below the wall that protects the Lungarno on this side, and this stretch of street is a high point on the waterfront. Looking upstream toward the Ponte Vespucci I hazard a guess that the water is about two feet below the span of the arch. There will be real damage done if the Arno should bring all this pressure against the bridges themselves. I wonder about the Ponte Vecchio up river at the centre of town, for the ancient bridge built by Taddeo Gaddi in 1345 is not strong and is very low; there was concern for that old landmark some years ago in the high water of November.

A yellow oil drum rolls past, floating half submerged, and then a whole series of playful grey and red gasoline cans, five-gallon size with spout tops. Some distributor's warehouse yard has been inundated and denuded somewhere up river. There is a long succession of these cans, which the river keeps bouncing like a juggler with a handful of coloured balls.

Logs, branches, two or three trees sweep straight down; and here near the shore the whirlpools grow stronger; they race back in foaming crests against the downpouring torrent from upstream. Lord, what a mess of litter! Half a dozen oil drums, crates, trees, all at once – a child's red ball, a window shutter turning slowly and sluicing ribbons of muddy water between its slats, a chair sailing serenely, its arms and carved back above water and holding steady and upright as if inviting someone to take a seat, then another chair, a little rickety one upside down, four spindle legs in the air. That means somebody's house up in the hills, no question about it.

Outside my window Dario, the *padrone* and cook, under a big black umbrella runs across the wide street and looks over the brick wall. He comes back slowly under the pelting rain, looking worried. It is high time to get dressed and find out what is going on. There is no hot water, so I wash sketchily, brush my teeth, and dress, pulling on a heavy sweater, for there is no heat, either. On an impulse for which I shall be grateful, I fill two big tumblers with tap water and set them away on a shelf. I throw open the windows, hear the wail of a siren, and shut them again.

The lobby is grey and tranquil, and everything seems normal and everyday: the Signora is standing looking calmly out of the great arched doorway toward the river, and Aldo, the curly-haired young *cameriere*, is mopping the marble floor, preparing for the day and the descent of the guests. The wide staircase with its marble balustrade and red velvet carpet curves up into the gloom, and there is no sound of movement in the little palace. I feel a strong sense of emergency, none the less. The Signora smiles at my concern. There has not been a flood in Florence since the eighteen-forties, and that one, like every year's high water, spilled out over the lowlands down river from the town.

'*L'Aro sempre contiene la piena,*' she assures me with confidence. It is the season of autumn rains, and the Arno must be expected to run full. She explains that there are dams upstream and that now some of the dam gates will have been opened to protect the upper reaches, but the high water is simply running through here to spill itself in the sea below Pisa. Her assurance, as I shall learn later, is common among Florentines, who have never in living memory known the Arno as a threat and are completely and tragically unprepared to deal with one when it comes. Outside, the rain falls with no sign of moderating. More oil drums float down.

By eight thirty the Signora begins to show concern, but not because of the rising and tumbling river; a far more serious matter is the right ordering of the household, and the bread for the *prima colazione* has not come. Albarosa, who is the secretary and the Signora's niece, calls the *fornaio*. The *fornaio* reports that there will be no bread; the cellar of the bakery is *lagato* and the flour is unusable. Now confusion is felt in the house. If the cellars are flooding with water, this misbehaving river is going to disrupt the right order of things; and the guests, who are gathering in the lobby looking for their breakfasts, begin to speculate rather excitedly on the possibility of a flood. Alberto, the second *cameriere*, is sent running out with basket and umbrella to another bakery. We go down the marble stairs of the entry to the big front doors to gaze at the river, which has certainly risen a foot or more in the last hour and is shooting up bursts of foam that hang in misty puffs in the air until the rain beats them down. The flotsam is thicker than ever, the whole river matted with straw, leaves, and logs.

In the middle of a tangle of green branches a drowned red-and-white cow goes by, head and stubby horns crowned with leaves. The cow is swept near the wall and goes round and round, waltzing dumbly in the whirlpool. In midstream crates sail high on the water, all wet new wood. Two bales of straw ride on a net of twigs, and now comes a poplar, a froth of green leaves, a long extent of half-submerged trunk, a mass of broken roots rearing up like a big spider's nest. An oil drum brightly enamelled in blue makes a splotch of colour on the muddy current.

Now a considerable amount of household furniture begins to mix with the masses of debris, and we feel a pang of worry for the people who must be homeless refugees up in the hills where all this water is coming from. A slender chair with fluted arms bows and curtsies, riding high with its padded seat out of water, a varnished stool, a green-painted kitchen table on a tilt, a stepladder, a desk, its drawers gone, a wooden clothes chest, a blue suitcase. Always oil drums, always brush and trees, and now there come two long painted beams with splintered ends which look like part of somebody's disintegrated house. Our uneasiness quickens as we realize that when this started, when the water rose in the night, the dwellers in this house whose beams and furnishings are racing seaward may not have been warned, may not have escaped; but nobody speaks this fear until a doll rides by on a mat of straw and a chatty American housewife of our number bursts out, 'Oh, dear, I keep looking for bodies and

I don't want to see them.' She earns a disapproving glance or two, but no one answers.

A huge steel tank easily fifteen feet tall and ten feet in diameter, battered by the bridges, tumbles and plunges and is followed by an old-fashioned wooden washtub with two of its slats squared off above the rim and perforated for handles. There is a great mass of indistinguishable litter and two tipsy pumpkins.

Alberto returns, breathless and grinning with excitement. There is no bread to be had anywhere, he reports; in the Prato behind us there is water all over the street. Here in the house the water taps above the ground floor have gone dry, and the pleasant-voiced professor from University College, Los Angeles, with a little amiable prodding, persuades Dario to fill the bathtubs on this floor while it is still possible. The gentle little Signora is worried chiefly because she can offer us only *pane casalingo*, the coarse grey bread baked in the kitchen, rather than the crisp white baker's rolls to which we are accustomed. Pots of hot tea and coffee take the chill out of our bodies, and half a dozen of us decide to brave the wild rain and find out what is going on at the centre of town.

Alberto warns us to stick to the Lungarno because of the water in the streets behind us to the north. Boots, raincoats, and umbrellas offer little protection against this storm. Rain falls in solid sheets, and we can see only fairtly and far off through the downpour the grey outlines of the Ponte Vecchio with its jumbled squares of goldsmiths' shops, the old bridge still standing through all this high water. The rain has covered both street and sidewalk with an inch-deep skim of water. Below the wall on our right as we walk, too close below the wall even here on high ground, the threatening brown river swells and tumbles, thick with debris and spume; and it roars. We have been vaguely aware of this deep rumble ever since the dawn. The youngest among us, a lanky young man in his twenties, sprints off ahead and disappears around a bend in the wall.

There are few persons in the street. Some look excited; those coming toward us from the centre look dazed. At the second bridge, Ponte alla Carraia, we come to a standstill, for looking east from the platform there, the short distance down toward Ponte Vecchio, we can see deep water in the street and, after a second unbelieving look, water pouring over the walls between the old bridge and beautiful Ponte Santa Trinita. The river is in the town.

We should have been prepared for all this, of course, after Alberto's warning about the water in the streets behind us, but somehow we were not. Shocked and feeling suddenly obtrusive, rather indecent – become curiosity-seekers, gapers, in a city encountering a catastrophe – we retreat, drenched to the skin, to the higher ground of the Lungarno Vespucci and our little palace, where we rub down and change in our chilly rooms

Those who did not venture out are upstairs in the big *salotto*, grouped at the three tall french windows; and they seem almost pleasantly excited; we find it impossible to communicate to them the grimness of what we have seen. We do not want to make things worse by talking of the danger that certainly exists, yet we are uncomfortably aware that the others do not understand what a mass of water is expanding in the streets of the city. But the rising flood outside tells its own story; the water is up another foot, perhaps two feet, it is hard to estimate; but it seems impossible, it is an absurdity that flood waters can rise like this, by feet in an hour or so rather than by inches as we seem to recall, from newspaper and television accounts that we have seen in the States, to be the normal behaviour of flooding rivers. The gravel banks across the Arno have nearly disappeared below the crest of the surging waters, whose tumult and velocity also seem greater. We begin to pray for this relentless rain to stop falling.

A number of cars are still crossing the high Ponte della Vittoria downstream from us and on our level, but toward the heart of town Ponte Amerigo Vespucci, Ponte alla Carraia, and Ponte Santa Trinita are closed to wheeled traffic. Around their piers our once-gentle Arno is raging like a sea in storm. A few human figures are hurrying across the bridges on foot. On Ponte Vespucci four rain-coated figures appear, trotting toward the other side of the Arno in a line, holding umbrellas before them at an identical cant. In their dark clothes they are picked out in the murk like people in a Japanese painting – the four black silhouettes bent forward, the black umbrellas, the brown water, the rain.

No arch shows any longer between Ponte Vespucci, the tide is leaning against the bridge itself, and the great tree trunks riding down strikes thunderously against the cement, throwing up a twenty-foot wash of water and a high cloud of spray that slowly drifts away. The water level crawls even higher.

By noon discretion prompts a little personal concern, and with the help of the boys my record player and records, my bags, an oil painting, and a few precious possessions are carried up to the *primo piano* and piled together in the big hall, with winter coats thrown over them – all this to the amusement of two transient guests, who haven't so much to lose.

Lunch at one o'clock is briefly reassuring in its opulence and variety, and we hungrily consume superb chicken *cacciatore* with three vegetables and find that a full stomach has restored our spirits considerably. Only the presence of the coarse bread and the absence of water pitchers remind us that we are not likely to eat so well again for some time. The radio has broadcast a warning that the city water is polluted; so we content ourselves with *acqua minerale* and wine, which are the standard Italian drinks anyway. There is still gas in the kitchen.

But over our cheese and fruit the talk becomes apprehensive. We try to find some news on the transistor radio the woman from Brooklyn has brought to the table and can get nothing but an insensate burst of dance music. Many of the Americans are impatient with what seems to them evidence of sheer incompetence on the part of the officials. Brief newscasts come over only at stated hours, and we speculate restlessly on the kind of coverage an American broadcasting station would be giving in such an emergency: there would be nothing but flood news, advice, instructions, reports, an uninterrupted stream of talk even when there was nothing new to talk about, with breaks for fuzzy voices coming in at intervals over portable microphones from reporters in every district of the town. But this is not America. It is easy to find fault, and we have no way of knowing that the Mayor, after a night of urgent organization of the city's forces, is marooned in the Palazzo Vecchio by rampaging flood waters and the Prefect, the national officer in charge of the Province of Florence and the source of authority for army forces and firemen, who also has been out all night, is cut off in the Palazzo Medici-Riccardi and that all telephones are out of service. We do know that our own telephones are no longer functioning.

Some of us who have transistors have heard a broadcast or two: the Santa Croce area is swamped, there is a metre and a half of water in the Piazza del Duomo, but as yet no houses have crumbled and no reports of deaths have come in. Our adventurous young friend who ran down clear past the borders of the flooded area reports a metre of water in the streets at Ponte Santa Trinita, and he keeps trying to make us understand how fast the water is running: nobody could stand against it, cars are being swept along and overturned. He wants us to take a look at the river out there and try to realize how furiously the water is moving in the streets.

We go back to our vigil at the windows of the *salotto*, realizing all too well that the emergency is growing worse, feeling sick with the knowledge of what must be happening to this elegant and beloved city, but with no concern in proportion to what is actually in store for her.

Of all the cities of Italy, Florence is the jewel – *bella Firenze* – the most beautiful, the most precious, the most intimate. Rome may be open and golden and rich with ruins from the days of the Caesars as well as with a superabundance of baroque; Venice may have her own floating fairy-tale loveliness and her oriental treasures; but Florence holds all the flavour, the finest works of art, all the prime flowering of the late Middle Ages and of the Renaissance within the compass of the 'old town', which lies along the Arno between Santa Croce and Ognissanti and stretches back only a few blocks from the waterfront. The centre that comprises the ancient city is small and compact. In those narrow streets and alleys and around those wide squares, frescoed and parapeted thirteenth- and fourteenth-century houses shoulder the handsome stone palaces from the days of Lorenzo the Magnificent, and the savour of those days of chief glory in the life of the city is not merely a historic remnant to modern Florentines, but an essence of the communal life. You stretch out a hand and the massive old stones are there, the marks of the artisans' chisels, the breathtakingly lovely vista, as you turn a corner, of the Arte della Lana from the year 1308 or the Palazzo di Parte Guella with its old battlements, its slanted staircase and Gothic windows, the curiously angled and almost windowless house and tower of Dante in a humble side street between the Palazzo Vecchio and Santa Croce.

Everywhere there are reminders that this was the city of Dante Alighieri:

*I' fui nato e cresciuto
sovra 'l bel fiume d'Arno alla gran villa.*

Engravings of his verses from the *Commedia* mark buildings that he knew and that his verses celebrate. The words *sovra 'l bel fiume d'Arno* are engraved on a marble plaque at the centre of the Ponte Vecchio above his beautiful river. In Borgo SS. Apostoli not two hundred yards away stands the shell of the house where the conspirators of the Amidei family in the year 1215 planned an assassination that initiated the bloody feud of Guelphs and Ghibellines and split all Tuscany for a century, and Dante's verses from the *Paradiso* identify the crumbling façade: many would be happy who now are sad if God had drowned the ambitious young Buondelmonte (who jilted his Amidei bride) in the river Ema the first time he visited the city. In this narrow street no larger than an alley, with its arching buttresses overhead shutting away much of the daylight, its solid Trecento palaces each built like a separate fortress with massive nail-studded doors and wrought-iron torch holders, past ages seem more alive than the present, and it is easy to picture the vain young bridegroom, dressed in white satin, riding over the bridge across the Arno on Easter morning, to be set upon and left lying in his blood at the foot of the statue of Mars – and the city suddenly in arms, house against house:

*O Buondelmonte...
se Dio t'avesse conceduto ad Ema
la prima volta ch'a città venisti.*

Florence: Ordeal by Water

In such arched and winding little streets Dante encountered his beloved Beatrice and grew faint with anguish when she refused him her salutation. The Baptistery is his beautiful Saint John's –*'mio bel San Giovanni'*; the *sasso di Dante* is the still-preserved stone where he used to sit to watch the workmen building the new cathedral, Santa Maria del Fiore, whose graceful bell tower Giotto designed.

Squares, churches, and palaces are still alive with incidents of the city's rich and tormented history, from the ring on the pavement of the Piazza della Signoria where Savonarola was burned to the vast grey-stone serenity of the cathedral nave, where the drama of the Pazzi plot of 1478 culminated – an attempt, probably with papal connivance, to overthrow the power of the Medici while the new heads of the house were young. The attack took place around the central altar, the signal being the elevation of the host at the most sacred moment of the mass. Handsome young Giuliano de' Medici, whose portrait can be seen in the lefthand figure in Botticelli's 'Primavera', was stabbed to death, while his ugly but brilliant brother, Lorenzo, fought his way to sanctuary in the sacristy, sword in hand. By nightfall the bodies of the conspirators were dangling from the windows of the Palazzo Vecchio, hanged by the neck, and the power of Lorenzo was solidified – that same Lorenzo who was to become the *Magnifico* and the patron of Renaissance genius.

Your modern Florentine is generally not very willing to give Lorenzo due credit for his share in cultivating that unmatched fervour of creativity in painting, fresco, and sculpture that brought Florence the glory of being both cradle and centre of the Renaissance, or perhaps the lustre of his genius as peacemaker and patron of the arts is befogged by the memory of all the sagging Hapsburg faces in the long generations of his heirs. 'Those Medici,' I have heard Florentines say with scorn, 'what did they know how to do? All they could do was make money. We had *artists* in Florence.' And artists they certainly had, many of the greatest of them born here, the others flocking in from other parts of Italy to take part in the creative ferment of the Quattrocento. This is the city of Giotto, Masaccio, the Gaddis, Donatello, Uccello, Ghirlandaio, Verrocchio, of Leonardo da Vinci, of Fra Angelico, of Fra Lippi and Filippino; and galleries, palaces, churches contain hundreds upon hundreds of their finest works. There are tombs, dwellings or workshops of such famous sons of Florence as Benvenuto Cellini, Andrea del Sarto, Sandro Botticelli, Niccolò Machiavelli, Galileo Galilei. Michelangelo, another Florentine, worked as a boy in the Medici Palace under the patronage of Lorenzo. Next to marble, Florence was Michelangelo's dearest love, and most of his finest statuary is here: the 'Slaves' and the 'David', the two great tomb groups in the Medici Chapel at San Lorenzo, the 'Brutus' and the 'Bacchus', several famous Madonnas, and two extraordinary late Pietà, to name only the most noted.

There is hardly a house, certainly not a church or palace in the ancient section that does not bear the memory or mark of one or more of these men. Brunelleschi's rosy dome crowns the skyline. Ghiberti's paradisiacal doors glow with gold under the morning sun. Orcagna's lacy tabernacle in marble mellowed to the tone of ivory is the chief beauty of Or San Michele, perhaps the most delicate and Gothic of the churches. Santa Maria Novella with its cloisters, the monastery of San Marco, Santissima Annunziata, Santa Trinita, Santo Spirito, the Carmine, and Santa Croce are treasure houses of art.

An enduring virtue of Florence is that her people display a dignity of bearing, a grace of manners, and an interest in scholarship in keeping with the omnipresent reminders of the antiquity and fame of their city, while in a mechanized century they keep alive the practice of craftsmanship, of the finest handwork in gold and silver, in leather, copper, onyx and marble, enamelled wood, copies of antique furniture, embroideries, fabrics, and high fashion.

Even the uninstructed female tourist on a shopping spree finds herself overawed, even shaken, and certainly bewildered among the thousands of elegant shops, which offer a choice of treasures of artisan make that she finds just too much for her. She may order a suit made, buy two gold necklaces, a handbag of *vitello or coccodrillo*, table linens, an antique chest of drawers, and then stand bemused and longing amidst the profusion of shops – very small shops, most of them, each offering the products of one craft only and all of exquisite workmanship. And as she walks and gazes, the spires and domes and monuments, the green and white marble, the massive stones of the Renaissance palaces, the predominant colour of the stuccoed houses of Florence – a rusty weathered gold – the frescoed walls, the lazy green river under its loops of bridges, all these begin to fill her with another and unfamiliar pleasure, the pleasure of perfect and congenial forms, for Florence was designed by men who built for the sake, first of all, of beauty. Once her charm takes hold of a visitor, no other city will again completely satisfy him.

And it is this city we are looking out on, this lengthening and tragic afternoon of the fourth of November, on her cypress-topped and villa-dotted hills across this rolling flood that is the Arno – just above us over the river the battlemented brick walls, *Le Mura di Santa Rosa*, a remnant of the protective fortifications that girdled the Florence of the twelve hundreds; farther uptown the pointed spire of Santo Spirito; on the hill above it the big white block of Forte Belvedere; and farther still and higher the graceful front of San Miniato and the green spread of the Piazzale Michelangelo, the latter now only a grey shadow under the falling rain.

Aldo comes in to report that the street behind the courtyard is running with water a foot deep, and the professor from Los Angeles rolls up his sleeves and determines that something must be done to save the cars that are parked on the gravel of the court within the heavy iron gates, gates that are all scrollwork on the street side but sealed within by solid sheets of steel. We go out back. The boys point with dubious, wry faces to three planks lying by an inner wall, not one of them long enough to cover the gap at the bottom of the doors, but the professor drags them out, none the less, and kicks them into place against the opening.

'If I had some sacks and a shovel I could make sand-bags,' he says, casting a wishful eye on the gravel of the courtyard. 'How the devil do you say *shovel* in Italian?"

'*Un badile*', I suggest, but no light shows in the Signora's eyes; apparently a *badile* is something that exists only on a farm. But suddenly she grasps the idea.

'*Una pala!*' she cries and hurries toward the kitchen, whence she emerges hopefully, bearing a rusty fireplace shovel with a five-inch blade and a short handle. But any shovel is better than none, and the professor sets valiantly to work. Now all the men have caught fire, and there is a large concerted effort to seal the gates. Aldo and Alberto bring wooden crates to scrape with and to carry the little piles of dirt and gravel, which are spilled into the cracks and stamped into place. Dario begins lifting down big flat roofing tiles from a pile alongside the gates, and these add height and strength to the barricade, which finally stands nearly a yard high and a foot thick. There are no more resources, and the little dike will have to do as best it can.

Back upstairs in the *salotto* we looked down upon a worsening prospect. The colour of the river has thickened to a dark, ugly brown, and the water is streaked with black and yellow oil, an incredible amount of oil like a scum on the tempestuous surface. It isn't bringing calm to these troubled waters whatever this oil is, wherever it can be coming from, wherever all those tons of water can be coming from.

One of the men puts on his raincoat again and runs down the staircase and across the street; he leans over the wall, thrusts down an arm, and brings it up with his hand dripping. A foot down, maybe, there is river. Moreover, there is the daunting consideration that the flood here must have been relieved to some extent by the water that is pouring into the upper town. We look at one another gravely, but not even the chatty woman loses control. A slender, bright-faced blonde woman, who carries with her a reassuring air of competence, says in a speculative tone, 'I wonder what this palace is built of. It looks all heavy stone on the street side, and it seems to me it's only those plaster affairs with crumbly mortar that give way under water.' We all gladly agree that the house is built of stone, though we are not at all sure of this. The professor's charming fair-haired wife radiates serenity.

By 3.30 the flood is lapping the top of the wall, and spouts of water like a dozen garden hoses spurt through apertures that are beginning to appear between the bricks. The flood is obviously reaching for us, and a few of us start putting on boots and raincoats for a last sortie, not as gawkers this time but from the pressing need to see with our own eyes the actual extent of the peril.

If a venture is to be made, it must be made now, for the wall is obviously threatened and the day is growing dark. '*Come fa buio a quest'ora,*' mutters Albarosa at her desk in the lower hall, where she has lighted a stubby candle against the growing gloom.

Our expeditions are not a communal affair; two or three persons will slip out together unobtrusively, or a man alone. Our lanky young man has been out in this for an hour already.

The rain has thinned to a drizzle. Past the piazza a block away, the Lungarno is covered by a three-inch layer of water; within the next two squares it becomes a mush of muddy water (with unexpected potholes), which splashes over the tops of galoshes every dozen steps. A helicopter goes over, flying low along the river, and somebody identifies it as belonging to the *Paris Match*, whose daredevil photographers will take any risk to get pictures, the first sign we have had that the outside world knows about Florence and her plight.

At Piazza Goldoni we are brought to a sudden halt. The Lungarno ahead is swept by a waterfall straight from the Arno, the wall buried under the raging force of the river except for the space of the brief rise to the bridge, where the emerging barrier tells our eyes but not our unbelieving minds that there is street under that full flow now moving inland to engulf the town.

Down in the piazza at our left, ten or twelve feet lower than the Lungarno at the bridge mouth where we stand, down the first narrow street back from the river, a mass of water is moving, pent wall to wall within the canyon of the buildings, smooth and swift, an enormous weight of water inexorably advancing. It fills the street three or more feet deep along the shop fronts and plunges down into the square with the ponderousness and rush of a waterfall. A little turmoil in this solid stream reveals the windshield and roof of a car skidding along fast under the push of the waters; it slides straight forward as if being driven, only its windows and top showing, then skitters sideways, is thumped against a wall and slowly overturns, its wheels reaching grotesquely, like the legs of a dog rolling on its back; then the water had it completely, and it goes tumbling over, showing a nose, a hump of roof, a flank, into the turmoil and uproar of the square.

In the square itself the broad cascade from the street explodes in a vortex of waves, whirlpools, and debris – branches, an oil drum, which it smashes against a wall, then against a shopfront – carrying too a float of twigs, shoes, pocketbooks, and paper, which swing round and round in a crazy bobbing dance. A strong current sweeps the car toward the shops – these sealed with great steel shutters because the day is a holiday – and slams it headfirst against a shutter, which shivers and begins to bulge under the battering. All the shops are taking a battering from the debris and from the heavily swirling water, and as we gaze in a sort of stupor we see that the two art galleries at the centre of the square are going to go, and very shortly; nothing can continue to take this for long. We turn our eyes away; we don't want to see it.

In endless onrush the waters pile in, the swamped square finding its outlet along famous Borgo Ognissanti. It is almost a straight sweep through from the flood pouring into the square and Ognissanti itself, now become a river racing onward toward the Prato, its entrance partially blocked by a jumble of upturned cars and leafy branches that makes the flood boil as it tears its way through and past. This flood in Ognissanti, now three feet deep and wall to wall, will race with nine to twelve feet of water before three hours are up, to continue to drum and roar at this damaging pace for eight or nine hours longer at full height, as the Arno, out of all bounds, washes higher and ever higher through the heart of Florence, until between midnight and three and in the morning the river will swiftly recede, leaving the city a waste and a shambles. But this we do not know as yet and will not know until tomorrow.

What shakes us and turns our stomachs sick is the irresistible weight and push of this onrush of water – brown water, incredibly bloated water – and its indiscriminate destructiveness. There are no words for the power of the Arno in the streets of Florence; we shall be told later that the speed of the river moving through the city is sixty kilometres hour, but at this moment we would not know how to deal with such a statistic; there is only the heavy flood coming on like water over a dam.

Heartsick, our uneasiness tinged with dread, we turn back along the Lungarno, sloshing through deepening water in the street, through which a strong current is beginning to run, so that we hasten our steps, pushing our way along, boots full and feet icy. There is much more water spouting through the weak spots in the retaining wall. Beyond the wall, the river is coming down against the Ponte Vespucci like an avalanche, butting against the superstructure and shaking it and then boiling back in a great rumpus of waves, which come on again harder than before. One of the iron railings has been cracked and wrenched askew.

Before we reach the high point where our little palace-*pensione* stands, the dirty tide is already beginning to creep along the street out front, and we join Dario, who stands impatiently at the huge wooden outer doors, waiting for the last foolish venturer to get back to safety. We watch him appear through the mist of the rain, a dignified elderly gentleman who was once an American consul general in Italy and who is fond of these people and feels a responsibility toward them. He goes in ankle deep between midstreet and sidewalk and comes slowly into the entry, shaking his head. In the open doorway our little Signora stands with her arms clutched against her waist, wailing softly, '*Quest'Arno, quest'Arno!*' as if reproving a delinquent child.

The great front doors are locked and the heavy bolt shot home, and Dario carries down an armload of sacks. The boys are removing the red velvet carpet from the stairs that go down to the entrance. At the back the courtyard is filling with water despite our brave little dike.

Upstairs in the *salotto* the tiny ancient *contessa* is having her tea in her usual armchair, and she is annoyed at the fuss. 'What has happened to the lights? It's very dim in here without lights,' she insists. 'And all these persons are talking extraordinarily loud. It is not necessary to talk so loud, is it?' We tell her that there is a flood, but she pooh-poohs the idea. She has known the Arno all her life, and it never floods. She is decided in her refusal to acknowledge any change in the established order of things, for she is a great lady of the old school, and her will is imperious. With her white hair, her soft skin and pink cheeks she looks like a dainty china doll circa 1900, but she will have no histrionics and declines to credit what we try to tell her.

Our lanky young man, home again and once more in dry clothes, reports any number of shop windows broken and the merchandise streaming away on the flood. He is angry with the shopkeepers. 'They aren't making an effort to save their stuff. That's the trouble with this fatalistic Italian attitude: they simply sit back and take what the good God sends, and the shops are suffering terribly, the stuff they have is all being ruined. Hundreds of cars are stalled by the water and the streets blocked with them.' Somebody who has been out suggests that salvage efforts might be a little difficult under present circumstances, but the lanky young man is obstinate in his vexation. He has seen two rats scuttling along the Lungarno, he tells us, and he rather cheerfully raises the possibility of plague.

The Contessa is finally drawn to the windows, where she looks down on the boiling Arno and the filthy inundated street, the flood now above the sidewalks and steadily climbing the retaining wall. 'But why don't they stop it?' she asks quaintly. 'What is anybody doing about it?' A number of American men agree with her. They want to know why there aren't sandbags; something could be done to hold this river in if there were enough sand-bags.

In spite of the rain, numbers of us keep going out on to the balcony of the *salotto* to get a better view up and down river, a full look at the street below. The small spouts of water coming through the wall have grown large, and in a number of places the bricks have given way and there are gaping holes through which the water pours as if from hydrants. The street below is now flowing as swiftly as the river – it is the river, only richer and darker in colour, covered by a heavy scum of black and chrome-yellow oil, a blotched blackish tide that looks as thick as gravy with mud and petroleum. Now we become conscious of a strong stench in the cold outer air. There is the sharp reek of oil; that, we have noticed for some time, but now it is mingled with the foul, sickish odour of putrefaction and the smell of sewer gas. The old sewers, blocked by mud and heavy flotsam, are regurgitating their unclean contents into the swamped streets.

Between our house and Ponte della Vitoria – down-stream, cutting us off as if on an island – suddenly we see the river sweeping straight in over the top of the wall.

It is not the hour for a news broadcast; nevertheless, we cluster around the big transistor on the table before the fireplace and twist the dial. Music, again dance music, and then suddenly a clear American voice begins discussing the defeat of Goldwater in 1964.

Already the water is coming in under the great front doors of the entrance three feet below the level of the floor of the downstairs hall, and guests and servants begin carrying mattresses and furniture up the wide, velvet-carpeted staircase. In half an hour the upstairs hall is piled full with these refugee pieces and with the suitcases and overcoats of the ground-floor guests. Our venturesome young man has inanely left two pairs of sodden oxfords on top of a cold radiator.

The professor reports that in the back courtyard the water is up to the fenders of the cars, but there is curiously little oil out there; the water has been seeping under our little dike and has not yet started to run in over it.

Before five the day has grown dark, and the Signora herself brings in two feeble candles and closes the shutters, and shortly Aldo appears with a pair of small kerosene lamps, which he places on the mantel. The great room is full of deep shadow, with four faintly glowing areas of illumination which pick out our whitish faces against the obscurity; it is only moderately cold. All at once bottles appear from suitcases on every hand, and everyone shares in a drink. There are Martinis on the centre table, there are bottles of Scotch and Hennessy, and there is mineral water, though of course no ice. But who wants ice? We stay close, we are caught in this together, with the river plunging into the streets outside, and the rather rigid social lines that have been preserved in the preceding days are spontaneously dissolved.

The talk grows noisy, though there is an undercurrent of agitation which the sound helps to drown. In an armchair near the windows our lanky man, who has waded so far and seen so much that is shocking and fearful, lies huddled in exhausted sleep.

The Italian news broadcast comes on at five. The chatterers are hushed, and the three of us who understand something of the language strain our ears to catch what we can from the rapid Italian voices on the air. We learn that Florence is isolated. All Tuscany is suffering from floods, and we are cut off by rail and road and telephone from Rome to the south and Bologna to the north. The heavy storm is general all over Italy; high winds have done damage in Sicily, in Naples, with huge trees uprooted on Capri. No help can reach Florence in this catastrophe.

Supper is served early, with two candelabra on the sideboard making a brave show but leaving the diners at the far end of the dining-room in shadow; and although the food is far less elaborate than the menu at noon, it is ample and hot. We marvel at Dario's skill and wonder how he has been able to provide such a feast, with supplies limited, the gas gone, and with no light but candle-light. He has fired an old coal stove in the kitchen and has cooked for twenty of us and for all the staff, using water from the house cistern, which stands well above the flood, has cooked with the water creeping up within inches of his kitchen floor, which is lower than the rest of the ground floor.

We begin making frequent journeys down to the lower hall, where Dario now stands guard over the rising waters in the entryway, already become a muddy pool two feet deep. The thin beam of a flash-light shows only one marble step still clear below the floor level. We go back up, we come down again, the water keeps rising, the step disappears under a brown film. The pool looks rather quiet, but having seen the power of the river that is now loose in the street out there, we feel some apprehension about the strength of the doors, though generally we regard the swelling water without talk and wait rather calmly. If this flood invades the house, and it will inevitably invade the house, there is nothing to be done about it. The margin of safety is four inches now.

At ten o'clock there is another news broadcast: Florence is a lake – an absurdly placid metaphor, this! There are three metres of water – that means ten feet! – in the Piazza del Duomo, and isolated families are calling for help from second-floor windows. All afternoon army helicopters from the parachutist brigade at Livorno have been rescuing people stranded on rooftops in the lowest sections of the city; only women and children have been taken; the men have been left on the roofs to wait for succour on another day. So that is what those helicopters were doing! Pisa is flooded. Pisa, which lies at the mouth of the Arno and is receiving the whole flow of the river, has sent Florence a message begging for help and has been refused. Florence cannot help herself.

All our faces are very sober now, and some voices are almost tearful, others are grim at the thought of the human misery and terror being endured on this black and drenching night. The talk dies. For those people isolated in the centre of the city it is a night out of the Middle Ages, without light, with no help available during the black hours, no voice to answer a cry. The people who are clinging to the ridges of their roofs cannot see the water rising in the dark, they can only dread it, themselves gone blind, and feel the rain pour down.

Uneasy as we may be, we are among the fortunate of the folk who are living this night through – perched on Ararat in this chill and hollow *salotto* in a dusk that is warmed by candle gleams, far above drowning Florence through the hours in which she is being ravaged by her own beloved river turned lion. We can get no more news at all from the radio. The Signora has instructed the boys to bring in the mattresses from the hall and make up pallets for us on the floor of the *salotto*, but no one is ready to go to bed yet.

Sometime between eleven and midnight a candle appears in the doorway of the *salotto* and above it Dario's face alight with good tidings. '*Scende,*' he calls out excitedly. '*L'acqua scende!*' The water is going down. We cannot believe it. We all pile down the stairs with our candles in our hands, and incredibly there is the wet and the oil mark on the wall of the entry showing where the flood reached and on the highest step bare inches from the floor, but the pool within the doors has shrunk, the water is down almost to the second step.

Our reaction is now a little shrill and anticlimactic. We offer stumbling congratulations to Dario as if he had himself checked the flood and saved the house from being inundated, and though he does not understand the English words, he catches some of our meaning from our faces and voices and responds with a wise shrug and a grimace. Somehow we never question that the worst is over, perhaps because we have been watching the water climb steadily for the past long eighteen hours and this peak is something we had almost given up hoping for. Perhaps it is the speed with which the flood is dropping or it may be sheer relief at our escape that won't let us contemplate the chance of anymore danger tonight. After the first few minutes there is a general let-down, almost a disappointment, in this harsh relief from strain.

'We got a good workout carrying all the furniture upstairs,' one of the men says ironically, and we laugh, because the failure of the flood to invade us has certainly robbed our salvage efforts of any special heroism. In our first breath of reprieve we are also conscious of a degree of wonder, as we look back over the preceding hours, that we have not felt more fear, that fear has been curiously suspended in us, with all our energy and attention sharply involved in the reality of what was going on. It was patent that the flood would take us if it were going to take us, and without having to stiffen our wills we discovered the basic truth of stoicism: that there is no arguing with an event one cannot control. With one or two brief exceptions no one has wanted to dramatize his plight with hysterics or been eager to welcome further catastrophe, even at a high pitch of tension. The danger has been too grave for folly and the woe we feel for this beloved city too full for dubious speculation.

But even yet we are a little reluctant to trust the behaviour of the river. The line that shows where the water came to is daubed on the entry walls – not two inches from the floor. Dario and the Signora tell us with determination that we shall sleep more restfully in our own beds than on mattresses laid out dormitory style in the *salotto*. The luggage is left heaped where we dumped it earlier, but mattresses and blankets go down the stairs, and the boys put our comfortable beds together. Dario will be our guarantee and will stand guard all night, and though we protest a little, we are glad enough to have him out there on watch as we snuff out our candle stubs and stumble between the sheets, feeling physically exhausted and emotionally spent. We sleep with shutters open, for no servant has thought to close them on this floor according to the peaceful routine of the house; and, alas, what intruder is there to fear; who could approach through that millrace out there in the street, along the overflowing river? In total blackness, heads sunk in our pillows, matches close at hand in case of emergency, we listen through waves of drowsiness to the roar of the Arno.

There is no memory of falling asleep, but hours later I am startled awake by a flare of headlights moving across the windows and hear the wet sloshing of tyres going by in the street outside. Relief floods me for the first time, and in the ensuing blackness I light a match to check the hour: three o'clock in the morning and that was a car in the street.

CHAPTER TWO

Desolazione

Saturday, November 5

When I wake again the window is rosy with sunrise and the sky is pale blue. I wrap a coat around me and fling open the windows on to a bright morning; a few light clouds above the spire of Santo Spirito are glowing with flame colour, and a diffusion of saffron light spreads outward from this burning centre and warms the pallid sky.

Across the Arno eroded banks and a strange high sand flat that was not there before paint a new landscape – and the flood is down, is down. The river has dropped a good eighteen feet in the night but is still a strong torrent, full of brown eddies and cross currents, very swift and still snarling wall to wall. A leafy tree slides smoothly down the centre of the stream, but there is relatively little flotsam this morning. On the new high sand flat almost at the peak of the opposite bank, one of the barges of the rock-crushing plant has come to rest far above the water. On this side, above the perforated but still unbroken brick wall, appear the tips of the trees of the riverbank, bent, stripped of leaves, and dripping black oil.

In this comfortable house there are now no comforts; the morning air is chilly in our unheated rooms, and there is no running water. I manage a cold sponge bath with a panful of water from one of the bathtub reservoirs, washing one area of skin at a time and rubbing down hard with a rough towel; and I find the shock of cold water and the ensuing glow quite invigorating; it brings back a summer on the Charles River and a summer in Maine, with our children squealing and jumping around us after a sharp dip in the dawn-misted water. Breakfast is plain tea and coarse bread without butter or marmalade, and we are glad to have it. Supplies of milk, butter, lemons, and other such luxuries are understandably unavailable this morning. Our cellar is flooded, the furnace drowned, and the oil tank floating; the jars of marmalade and the reserve supplies of wine bottles lie deep under muddy water. Yet we are a long way from suffering hardships, having a roof over our heads, warm beds with dry blankets, and a hot teapot to cheer the start of the day. The people in the streets all around us are coming down the stairs of their houses from the upper floors, where they huddled for a sleepless night, to gutted kitchens, splintered furnishings, cold, mud, and hunger.

In small parties we make a first sortie, joining the groups of silent Florentines who are moving along the Lungarno in a sort of daze toward the centre of the city. There is oil mixed with mud in the gutters, but wind and morning sun have so far dried the street that I very nearly put on rubbers instead of galoshes. I join the former Consul-General and his wife, and we follow the wall along the river, where there is less mud than on the far sidewalk. It is to be a day of shock, the walk a mounting revelation of desolation and despair; and each shock is fresh and incredible; one scene of devastation does not prepare us for the next.

The extent of the tragedy of Florence reveals itself gradually at first. We see the torn bridge ahead, heaps of detritus caught between its warped railings and a big stack of oil drums filling the near end. By the time we reach Ponte Vespucci we are walking in thick slime, a slippery blackish-brown paste that forces us to tread flat-footed to keep from sliding, and Mrs. Consul-General decides to turn back for fear of falling, but we two will go on. We cross the street, to where the handsome palace fronts display a coat of black oil to the height of the flood water, and as we progress, this line climbs steadily higher and the mud grows thicker underfoot. In the wide entrance hall of one of the palaces a porter is sweeping liquid mud toward the sidewalk with an old broom, but the muddy soup in the hall behind him is five inches deep and the little path fills up again as he moves along, though the additional paste on the sidewalk shows that he has been at his task for some time. We tread around it.

Here is the iron grille work covering the window of a fashionable dress shop, but there is no glass behind it, and on the floor inside in six inches of dark water lie overturned counters, a mass of sodden mud-soaked boxes and garments – a complete waste. Oil daubs the wall for two feet above the water on the floor. Just beyond, an unbroken small show window displays a pair of spike-heeled blue dancing pumps with silver buckles, still pristine on a white satin pillow.

The farther we go, the more the destruction increases, hardly a shop is intact, every courtyard is a swamp of mud. In the morning sun the city is ominously still.

At Piazza Ognissanti, where the Grand Hotel faces the Excelsior, we look down on a frightening mess. A black mat of oil covers the façade of the beautiful little church almost to the tops of the doors, and there is a marsh of mud, rotten straw, and litter a foot deep piled in undulations across square and street, in which battered cars, coated brown to the roofs, are jammed together as if in mammoth collision. Porters in boots are scraping and sweeping out a fifteen-inch sludge of muddy water from the lobby of the Excelsior, and there is a ladder on the Lungarno side stretching from the sidewalk up to the second-floor balcony, to permit the descent of guests of the hotel.

One block farther on, at Piazza Goldoni, there is complete devastation. The square is a nightmare tangle of cars, branches, mud, uprooted paving stones, and ruined merchandise. The big pharmacy on the western corner stands black and gutted, its three huge steel door-shutters crumpled like so much paper, shelves and counters collapsed in a splintered, mud-thick mound four feet high, among which befouled little squares of drug boxes and broken bottles are sprinkled like thick confetti. And the oil covers everything. Where did it come from, we ask, this tide of petroleum? As high as the water reached, streets and sidewalks, outer and inner walls, sodden merchandise, tree branches, straw, rubbish are thickly tarred with it. The two art galleries, Galleria Goldoni and Galleria Masini, are heartbreaking. Nothing is left on the smeared walls, the grilles twisted, the glass gone; and in a heap of broken and gummy squares on the floors lie the handsome canvases we have stopped to admire, passing on a happier day; all is half buried in black slime. The little streets leading into the square are similarly heaped, littered, and oil streaked. The centre of beautiful Florence is a forlorn wasteland. Palaces and shops gape empty; the long stretches of blackened building fronts look as if a wall of fire had swept through and left them charred and sooted. The city is empty – empty of all save ruin.

The people of the city who are gathering here in small groups stand gazing in stupor; there is no protest on the faces, there are no gestures or cries, there is only shock and deep pain. *'Che disastro!'* a grey-haired man cries out in a voice shaken with incredulity, and an echo made up of misery and astonishment runs through the crowd of watchers. All along the Lungarnos, moving slowly and heavily as if each step brought an ache, the procession of silent Florentines passes, halts, stirs again. The faces of these crowds will never leave our memories – the astounded eyes, the mouths distorted with distress, the disbelief and the stunned realization.

We move to the bridgehead, from which we looked down into the square only yesterday when the flood was rising, and our eyes are stricken by a new scene of destruction. The wall ahead along the river is broken and gone, all the way to Ponte Santa Trinita; the paving of the Lungarno is torn away in six-foot blocks; and the street is heaped with these and with waves of sand and mud, uprooted streetlamps, glass from windows, bricks, water pipes. From the demolished masonry here and there trail shattered electric cables, their torn ends forming a weird frowzy fringe along the edge of the ruined street.

The piers of the bridge, as we pass beyond it, are deeply indented where massive blocks have been torn away, the broken stonework matted high on the upstream side with trees, straw, smashed furniture, and with one great fold of red-painted steel which has wrapped itself around the rest of the litter in an embrace.

It is almost impossible to pick our way around the gaping pavement and heaps of detritus toward Ponte Santa Trinita. Deep troughs are gouged out everywhere; the marks of water and oil on the building fronts are six feet high. The famous print shop of Fratelli Alinari is a ruin, all glass gone, metal shutters twisted and fractured, counters and prints – except for a clean and beautiful half dozen high on the walls swept into a jumble in a mass of sand, water, and black oil wall to wall – a witch's brew of destruction. A once handsome white Mercedes convertible lies crushed against a shop front. The river front is strewn with trees and branches, and the wire grilles on the windows are mats of grass, straw, and twigs. Across the Arno the watermark draws a line above the first floors of the houses.

As we approach Ponte Santa Trinita, we see leafy branches of trees fluttering above the centre of the bridge on the far side, trees that have broken deep gouges in the massive piers and become lodged in the gaps in the stone and now flicker in the sunlight with a false air of festivity.

Before us along the riverside a vast gap appears. Halfway along towards Ponte Vecchio there *is* no Lungarno. The whole street, except for a thin strip along the buildings, has crumbled into the river, where the flood, plummeting over the block of the ancient bridge, whirled back on itself and ate away walls, masonry foundations, and river front. On the near end, where part of the street remains, the pavement has been peeled off like a rind. Inland the streets stand in water, black and void; and this is the heart of the gutted town. Is it possible that water can have done all this? '*O povera Firenze,*' a man of aristocratic bearing mutters, and his mouth quivers. Oh, poor Florence.

We do not see the buildings we are passing; we only stumble along the torn waterfront with our eyes fixed, now on the uncertain footing, now on the Ponte Vecchio. The old bridge stands but it is blasted; the goldsmith's shops are black shells, backs and fronts torn away by the waters, which broke straight through them, carrying everything away. Some of the goldsmiths were warned during the dark hours by their own night watchmen, who telephoned to say that the old bridge was going; and families drove down in haste through the black streets and the rain, to remove the most precious of their stocks of gold and diamonds, selecting hurriedly by candlelight, while the bridge shuddered and quaked underfoot and threatened to collapse at any moment. But there were many who were not notified or who could not reach the bridge in time, and this morning these pitiful people are on their knees, crawling among the incredible clutter of mud, branches, and trash, scraping away with their bare hands, sifting the mud and wet sand, to discover here a chain, there a ring, here a small pin, which they lift up with an air of incredulity that is almost pleasure – something saved from the loss of the whole investment of their patrimony – prosperous merchants become scavengers. All the rest is down in the Arno.

The street on the town side, Por Santa Maria, is a sea of mud and rubble, and further heaps of refuse are beginning to accumulate on the sidewalks, for the men and women of the shops are already here and are at work, mud to the waist and often to the shoulders, with brooms and shovels, starting the endless labour of cleaning out.

We watch as they push and shovel out of their doors, not only little mounds of the muck and sand that have accumulated with the flood, but the once handsome goods that were their stock in trade: mud-drenched art books, gummy and sodden handbags and shoes, oily ribbons that were once silk blouses, dresses, and lingerie. On to the sidewalk or into the gutter it all goes, torn and spoiled beyond any hope of saving. The shop people work with still faces but with relentless determination. None of them weep. Early this morning when they first laid eyes on the devastation of their city, they stood with tears running down their faces, for her sake and for the loss of all they owned; but the people of Florence have had a long schooling in adversity, and at once they set to work, quiet, stubborn, resolute, tackling a job that is just too big to be done.

A heavy-bodied woman in a blue jumper pauses in her sweeping to rest, leaning on her long broom and wiping the sweat from her forehead with the back of her arm. The man and woman from the next doorway come out to speak to her. Italians like to show feeling by touching each other, and one puts a hand on her arm, the other pats her shoulder.

'*Terribile*,' the man says in a voice thick with grief, and the woman in blue answers, '*Terribile!*'

'Worse than the war,' the man says heavily, and the woman weighs his words and answers, 'Yes, the war was nothing like this.'

'Destitution,' the man says, gazing along the horror of the street, and the women nod dumbly, touch each other again, and go back to their labours with the same composed faces.

We stand, gazing with growing amazement at these obstinate, mud-splattered people. There are only one or two of them at work in any one shop, and half the shops are still untended, bashed in, filled with waste, desolate. Those who are here are grubbing away at knee-deep to hip-deep trash and befoulment, digging at the mud or probing through the mess to pick out and set aside to save an unbroken shelf or drawer from among the splinters. One man is trying to scrape off the thick gum of oil from one of these salvaged pieces with a fragment of lath he has rooted out of the general destruction. The task is wholly beyond their powers, and their efforts appear to be making no impression at all upon the monumental filth and clutter, yet their faces are set and the old brooms swish away doggedly. The Consul-General is a grave and undemonstrative man, but his voice has grown harsh with astonishment and pain.

'This is ruin', he says, 'it is simply ruin. These little businesses are wiped out; everything is gone. I don't see how they'll ever be able to start again.'

The police, very wisely, are now beginning to turn away all pedestrians from the neighbourhood of the old bridge except for the shop owners, and on our way back along the river we pass a large shop of marble statuary, all the glass gone, its interior a rubble of brick and stone, headless statues, oil and water. A woman wearing a sweater but without boots is spilling out little shovels – full of mud and sand beneath the ragged wire mesh of the shop front.

Back at Ponte Santa Trinita my companion and I part ways, because I want to cross the square; and he is wiser than I, for the area below the bridge is impassable, a pond of muddy water two feet deep. I plod around the edge but am cut off and essay a roundabout path along Borgo Santissimi Apostoli, a narrow thirteenth-century track, where I slog through mire four inches thick and skirt overturned cars crumpled against walls in a way that is barely wide enough for a single car to get through when traffic is moving, until I find an alley leading north. The alley looks treacherous; it is almost two feet deep in swamp, but the mud lies on top of a bank of sand and may be navigable. I test each footstep, drawing back quickly when the sand begins to yield, and I am in up to the tops of my galoshes every few steps. The only litter here is a long line of women's shoes – from some good shop, though there is nothing good about them now, so mud-drenched that my first momentary impression is that women walking here have lost their shoes to the bog in the alley. A woman and child enter the alley from the other end but withdraw quickly as their feet begin to sink. A few long risky strides, and I make it, legs splashed with mud and a trickle of water seeping down around my heels. To the left again, sliding past a jam of overturned cars and a demolished motor-cycle, and I am in Via Tornabuoni above the pond in the square.

Via Tornabuoni is the most elegant of the great shopping streets of Florence; it is Fifth Avenue at Fifty-seventh Street in an Italian setting, and it is an empty desolation. There is no sound except for an ambulance siren which wails away somewhere to the north and fades out of hearing. Hollow shops, building fronts grimy and foul with oil, emptiness, ruin. In this lifeless street one or two persons stand staring, not moving. To my right the shrubbery and graceful wire chairs of a sidewalk café are an oil-dark tangle like a thornbush, festooned with strings of blackened paper and straw. In this terrible silence, the heart of Florence seems to have stopped beating. This has always been a noisy and lively city; it is impossible to imagine life moving here again.

Across the street, beyond a mound of debris, bricks, rubble, and mud, a sign reads: WAGON-LITS COOK, and the wire grilles over the windows are matted thick as doormats with grass, twigs, streamers of sodden paper. A little way along, in the very centre of the empty pavement lies a great tree, a strange intruder in this avenue of lost elegance. I can hardly credit the length of it and begin to pace it off, counting three feet to a stride, and it is forty-five feet long! As I stand staring, I hear a voice calling my name, though this hardly seems likely. A hand clutches my arm; it is the woman from the tailor's shop where the night before last in the driving rain I went to have a fitting – it seems ages ago! She is dressed up as if for a Sunday outing, but her shoes and legs are covered with mud. She stares desperately into my eyes, her face dark with grief but wholly contained.

'*O Signora,*' she cries, and she hangs on to me as if to a floating log on the flood, '*il negozio è tutto andato, tutto andato!*' I can well believe it, for I have just seen the spoiled street by the Ponte Vecchio where the shop stood. For a few minutes we cling to each other, talking in broken, desolate phrases, for there is nothing to be expressed but sorrow, and she cannot allow herself tears; I am closer to crying than she is.

'*Non c'era pre-allarme,*' she says with tension in her voice. She is a handsome woman, dark-eyed and young, and her muscial Florentine voice recounts in all the low changes of a lament the poor story of the passing of the little shop. It was because of the lack of warning that nothing was saved; they live on the other side of the river, and by the time they learned of the flood, around nine in the morning, the area near Ponte Vecchio was already a trap of moving water. A niece who lives on this side of the Arno came down in haste but had to flee before the oncoming torrent. And all the garments finished for customers or in the process of making, all the bolts of silks and fine woollens were reduced to strings and tatters soaked with slime and petroleum. It is a *finimondo*, she says with pained resignation – an 'end of the world', the extreme Italian term for a catastrophe. I hear the word on many tongues this morning, but I shall not hear it again after today, when the people of the city have endured the first shock, the first full blow of this devastation; the term is too final and suggests a surrender, and even on this first morning it is becoming apparent that stricken Florence is not going to surrender.

Farther up Via Tornabuoni, where the open front of one of the big bookshops exposes a mass of pulp spread over the floors, in a high window a slim pink volume beams out with a clean face, its title announcing cheerily that *La felicità è un cucciolo caldo* (Happiness is a warm puppy) – Charlie Brown indomitably riding out the flood.

East from the Strozzi Palace there are more watchers in the streets, more shopkeepers at work trying to clean out the mess, though the mess is so appalling that here too it looks as if they are accomplishing nothing. Those who have them wear boots, some men are in waders, many have their feet and legs encased in plastic bags wound round with string. Everyone who is working is mud to the waist. Strangers speak to each other and clutch at each other to point out particular horrors in the scene of destruction. '*Che disastro!*' they say, flinging out desolate hands. These people too look stunned.

On one street corner there are accusations, a heated discussion of the failure of the city to give an alarm. Why weren't the bells rung, the old alarm bells of the Palazzo Vecchio? Why wasn't the city alerted by sirens? A big man in a handsomely tailored topcoat says wryly that if the sirens had been sounded the people would have thought an atomic attack was coming and everyone would have run to the cellars – not the safest refuge from a flood – and a slow smile goes over a number of faces, a shadow of the old Florentine spirit of mockery. Another voice says that a general alarm would have produced a traffic jam as the merchants drove in to try to save the goods from the shops, and hundreds of persons would have been caught and drowned along with their merchandise; as it was, the lack of alarm and the fact that the day was a holiday saved many lives. The cars of those who came into town early for the *festa* created congestion enough; cars of those who heard the early fire sirens and drove down were stalled and stranded – and here indeed they are, many of them on the sidewalks wrecks of cars, wheels off and bodies smashed, or cars miraculously whole but plastered with oil and dripping muddy water.

Along Via Vecchietti, a street of commercial and savings banks, there is thick black oil in the gutters, but the black smears on the buildings are only four feet high though high enough to have left the banks swamped (Il Credito Italiano found a heavy tree trunk in its foreign-exchange lobby) and the *botteghe* badly damaged. The worst destruction was wrought in the low-lying streets parallel to the river where the full tide poured through; many cross streets, though badly hit, did not suffer from so high a flow of water. Here three broken windows are already boarded over. In the china shop where I bought crystal glasses only last week, the windows are still whole but the doors must have given way, for the floor is splattered with shards of Minton, Staffordshire, Dresden, Royal Delft, and Sèvres and Waterford glass. The porcelain and crystal left on shelves and tables wear a blackish-brown scum, and the carpet is a dark pool of slime.

Above the mud on the sidewalk outside a shop door stands a rack of mushy neckties, dripping oil. In a pet-shop window hang cages of drowned songbirds.

In the Piazza della Repùbblica the *carabinieri* have already erected a big wooden shelter, but the square looks as if it had been hit by a hurricane rather than a flood, for it is streaming with sodden paper – ribbons and mats and sheets and thousands of scraps of paper plastered everywhere and wreathing the jumble of branches, filthy chairs, and shattered tables which are all that is left of the fashionable cafés where one could once sit for hours in the sun, reading a newspaper or magazine and sipping a *cappuccino* or a Cinzano.

The *galleria* where the florists' stalls stood, on the west side of the piazza, is massed with mud, debris, and cars that have been washed into the arcade, all covered with a funerary strewing of bedraggled flowers, ferns, greenery and sprinkled with broken lamp bulbs.

And the oil, the oil! There is not an object or an inch of flooded wall that is not daubed with this reeking fuel oil, in some places inches thick. It looks as if it could never be got off; it looks as if a lighted match could burn the whole town down; but this is a city of stone and every inflammable object is so water-soaked that perhaps this is an unwarranted fear. (Long after, I learn that the firemen were on the alert for weeks because of the danger of fire from the heavy coating of fuel oil on the town.)

Even worse than the water and mud, it is this oil that has put the finishing touch to the damage to goods and furnishings. On the way to the Duomo I pass a shop of fine leathers, where in the window a red calfskin bottle blotched by oil has fallen on its side and where on the sidewalk I nearly stumble over a sticky heap of fine handbags in snakeskin, calf, and suede, wallets and purses, oil-drenched and half buried in a deep paste of mud – refuse! A muddy broom stands over them leaning against the shop front. I know the shop and its goods – of finest artisans' work, these rotting bags would have sold for from thirty to seventy dollars apiece and would have brought twice the price in the States. The losses are incalculable; most of the shops are small private enterprises with all their resources invested in their stock, and in most cases these piles of discarded goods must indeed mean destitution. How do you start again when there is nothing left to save? When you are already in debt to the bank for merchandise that can never be recovered?

But slowly and patiently in all these streets, here are the Florentines already starting again, if only to discard their losses and get their heads above the mud, and it is an admirable thing to see. From almost every doorway, shop door, or house front comes the patient swish of brooms and the scraping of shovels, old brooms and inadequate shovels, but from carpets and marble floors they are unweariedly scraping the liquid mud, and when too much mud accumulates on the pasty sidewalks they begin sweeping them as they are accustomed to do in fine weather when they make everything ready for a day's business. Now their means are insufficient by far: their tools are puny, there is too much mud and muck, there are mountains of it. (When over a month later I read the engineers' reports that on this day drowned Florence lay buried under 500,000 tons of mud, the figure seems just and the estimate no more than moderate.)

And to make the task of removal impossible, there is no water; the aqueducts are broken, and the only water lies out there under that heavy coating of oil, a thick muddy slop. How can they ever get rid of this filth without water? And where can the mud go? The narrow slits along the kerbs that are the entrances to the choked sewers cannot take it. Just now it is going into the streets, the heaps from the shops and houses building higher the piles of gummy refuse, cars, trees, shattered counters and furniture, and paving stones which are already cemented together by the mud the flood lodged here. The progress in cleaning out is infinitesimal, but there are no other means of restoration, only private hands, one pair of hands for so much mud in so many hours, and nobody sits down in resignation or pause to lament. I suppose that if they really started calculating possibilities, they would be brought to a stop; so they don't calculate, they just shovel. No, I am wrong to say so. There is nothing blind or stupid about what is going on here.

It is an error to underrate the solid realism of these people, who have always had to live close to the line of safety and who do not delude themselves. They are making no mistake about the magnitude of the disaster that confronts them. The man in Via Porta Santa Maria who cried 'Destitution!' was making a sober appraisal of the common plight. The amazing thing is that in the face of this knowledge the people are steadily going to work instead of sitting down and howling their woe, as they must be tempted to do. They continue to shovel and sweep. In the end, these are the people who will save Florence – who dare to attack chaos with a broom.

Although by this time I have become somewhat accustomed to horrors and even though the radio reports last night should have prepared me for what I was about to see, the sight of the Piazza San Giovanni is a terrible blow. The vast square is barren – a waste. The doors of the cathedral are shut, and the square is a no-man's-land of dislodged paving stones, tree branches, rags, snapped-off street signs and traffic markers, uprooted iron poles and chains, all lying in the muddy open. The oil is very thick here.

Unbelievably high, between the huge green and white marble Duomo and Giotto's belltower, a green car is jammed and mangled, a small damaging item of the flood's discard. On one ancient Roman sarcophagus before the south doors of the Baptistery an oil drum is lodged. A small crowd has gathered around the Baptistery, and I draw near, joining the first group of watchers. Over the heads I see that the wooden inner doors at this side of ingress have been broken open and shattered. But the Pisano doors? Their bronze framework has disappeared, and one of the squares of bronze relief from the lower side of the right-hand fourteenth-century door is not there, there is only a dark hole. One Italian says in a low voice that fragments have been found. It was the plaque representing charity.

There is an even larger crowd on the western side of the Baptistery, where stand the glorious Ghiberti doors which Michelangelo named 'the doors of Paradise'; but I have still felt no dread, I am still labouring under the delusion that the flood must have entered the square from the south, the side closest to the river; whereas the heaviest onrush of water, as the high-stranded car might have told me, came down the streets parallel to the Arno, from the east. Oh, dear God, not these doors! But there are five gaping blanks where the ten marvellous panels hung, and an officer is directing two policemen to lay the last of the five great torn-out plaques on top of the pile of the others. There is a small restless movement in the crowd. I am anything but an aggressive person, but I find that I have pushed through to the protective grille, and under compulsion I call out softly to the officer in charge (it is very silent except for the slight ringing of the metal), 'Are they damaged? Are they damaged beyond the loosening and the *nafta?*' The police officer turns a stern face to gaze at me, his eyes fill with tears, and he nods but he cannot speak.

We are moved to one side as the cart appears that will carry away these panels, which are numbered among the rarest treasures of art, not only of Florence, but of the world. We watch as if spellbound. A man who looks like a professor says quietly to his companion, 'To think that during the war, when the Germans were coming, we brought in the best artisans and art experts from all over Italy to remove them, to save them from the *Tedeschi* – and they couldn't get them off, they couldn't loosen them!'

I plod off, feeling sick and weary, thinking What about all the rest of the art? What about the Medici Chapel at San Lorenzo? The Michelangelos at the Academy? The Bargello? What about the frescoes? The paintings in the churches? After this shock I am suddenly leaden with fatigue, and I wonder how the Florentines, whose treasures these are, can stand it, for I, who am not a Florentine except through affection, at this moment am sick with grief and I can't take anymore. It isn't right, I say angrily to the heavens, it isn't fair. I feel cold to the bone and enraged rather than tearful.

There is a short cut home by way of the railway station, which lies two long blocks away – or there was a short cut two days ago – and I make my way, sliding and clambering along the blocked streets, clutching building fronts and climbing over high mounds of muck and debris, past weird tangles of fallen steel shutters, heavy brass grilles wound into twisted skeins of metal, splintered shelves, and furniture – all festooned with foul rags, straw, and matted paper. Via Cerretani is a junk heap of cars – fenders, tops, and doors bashed in; a blue hardtop which has been rolled over and over and crushed flat blocks the narrow sidewalk, its upholstery ripped out and hanging out the rear-window space, the whole body crumpled, windshield gone, battery dangling, motor split, wires laced with rags and weeds.

In the narrow street leading to the station, the shops have been inundated almost to the ceilings, gratings are broken outward as the flood gushed back out of the swirling interiors, wide areas of pavement have been ripped up. These are mostly modest shops that cater to the general populace, and lines of low-priced dresses and suits hang dripping filth along both sides of the street. The muck underfoot is dangerously laced with broken glass. In front of a *pellicceria* sopping furs hang out in the open like poor drowned cats. The faces of these people are haggard, and the eyes with which they regard the passers-by are dulled by desperation and the hopeless endurance of loss.

In the station square the watermark is six feet high, and loose bricks and paving stones make the footing perilous. The station itself stands above the height of the flood, but the path of the water can be traced along the rows of shrubbery and blasted cannas of the gardens that line the rise; dead bushes that look as if they had been dipped in tar give place near the peak of the gardens to a higher line of green and flowering red.

Groups of the curious stand around the entries of the two long pedestrian underpasses in the square, and the picture of how the flood must have gushed down into underground channels, sucking with it everything in its path, is painted in black evidence on the deep lakes that were the entrances to the ramps, where the worst entanglement yet of logs and topsy-turvy cars thrusts up through a bog of petroleum and drowned trash. Down in the underpass, shops and coffee bars line the walkway, and the word goes through the knot of spectators that twenty-four persons were either trapped down there as the water rushed in from both ends or were swept off their feet in the upper square as the current poured into these cul-de-sacs and were borne below and drowned there. There are rumours everywhere, and it is hard to know what to believe, but the broad entrances jammed high with upended cars and trees are proof enough that the tide carried everything portable along with it and that any unlucky walker in the square would have been helpless to save himself from the force of the suction. '*Venti-quattro persone sepolte*' the murmur goes from mouth to mouth '*Era una trappola.*'

Bright sunlight lies over the bleak landscape, and I climb in warm sun toward the station and walk across the marble platform within, now laced with long mud tracks from the feet of passers through. No one is waiting for a train, for there are no trains, the countryside around us lies under broad miles of lake.

On the far side of the station only a few short blocks separate me from the Lungarno, but after one attempt it becomes apparent that there is no way through to the river. Between lies the depression of the Prato, and the Prato is a sea of brown water, on which rubber boats are being propelled by rescue crews of firemen, bringing bread and water to the people marooned on the upper floors of the houses, whose ground floors are still deep in flood water.

I trudge wearily eastward, trying one cross street after another, only to be turned back by flooded streets or waved away by booted men on the edges of the drowned areas. I pass a bakery, identifiable by a two-foot-deep gum of filthy flour and meal on the sidewalk, through which protrude mangled utensils and a pair of broken scales. So many intimate small objects are scattered through the mud that they bespeak a thousand private tragedies – a child's skates, a long trail of red-and-black typewriter ribbon, an oil painting, a nightgown, a pair of bent eyeglasses.

As I turn back from the third cross street, a well-dressed young Italian in rubbers accosts me and asks whether it is possible to get through. The booted men look at our feet and laugh grimly, and we throw out our hands and move away. The young man has walked down from his house far up in the hills at Fiesole, for he is gravely concerned for the safety of his brother's family, who live across the Arno, and there is no way to reach them but on foot, if this can be done. He grows more and more shaken as we make our slow progress through the ruin of street after street. He is frightened because he was unable to telephone to his brother, who lives in a low district; there are young children in the family. Yet he maintains a grave and courteous demeanour and helps me over the worst mud holes, as if we were acquaintances making a pleasant *passeggiata*.

I think back on the many examples of graciousness and good breeding that I have met today, the more revealing because Florentines can be curt and are by no means generally patient. There has been, not only no hair tearing, but no harshness; there has been rather a grave restraint, a dignity that was able to meet even total disaster without heroics, a concern for the figure one cuts and concern for the grief of others which has forced a quiet masking of each one's private pain and the putting on of a brave face, in which only the revealing eyes are pools of desperation.

Bisogna fare la bella figura is a rule of Florentine life that has not always seemed admirable to me, but today's composure in the face of tragedy is a proof that ceremoniousness is not the least valuable of the fruits of civilization, that a common observance of docorum may be a bond of strength among a people.

Far up Via della Scala stand the army barracks, and here we encounter the first signs of help arriving for the stricken city. Cars and trucks are rolling in, loaded with soldiers in field dress and camouflage uniforms, but there seem to be no orders, and the soldiers look around them with broad curiosity as they jump down from the trucks and gather in idle groups in the street. A lieutenant comes out of the gates and directs one lot indoors.

We are on high ground once more, but when we reach the tree-lined avenue that leads to Ponte della Vittoria and the river, we find it just barely penetrable, for the sides are deep in swamp and cluttered for blocks with cars and trucks piled on top of one another in massive, flood-created collisions – car bodies foul and dented, doors and tops gone. A big grey dump truck has folded up a red SITA bus like a punctured football. It is possible to walk only in the tracks of the cars that have passed on their way to the bridge, for everywhere else the mud is so slick with oil that every step brings a skid.

A few cars are passing, but at a cautious speed, very unlike the customary breakneck Italian way of driving, and we slide to the side away from them, but the tyres spew out a wide fan of slush which catches us at the knees. Oh, well, nobody is keeping clean today in Florence. My coat is long since grubby, my gloves oil-daubed; my companion's trimly creased trouser legs are spotted and the turn-ups plastered.

I have to wade the last block to the Lungarno, slipping and sliding through endless pools of sludge and grease. Then here at last is the sunny waterfront, silent, empty, and forbidding, with below the wall the brown scour and rumble of the still powerful river. A helicopter roars by along the Arno, flying low.

Our little palace is full of news and rumours. The big hotels are all closing – the Grand, the Villa Medici, the Excelsior, the Anglo-American – their kitchens and heating plants under water, their ground floors a marsh of mud, no services possible since light, food, and water are all unavailable. The professor's wife, who has been to the American consulate, reports finding crowds of tourists there trying to get away. Some of them, she reports shamefacedly, want to buy their way out, as if money could make that much difference when the trains can't run, when the Autostrada del Sole is still *lagata* and the outer world shut away from us.

The news of damage in the city is grave. The beautiful churches have suffered terribly, with losses of incomparable masterpieces of frescoes, paintings, and sculpture. The foundations of the Duomo are weakened and its pavement buckling, and no one is being allowed to enter; Giotto's *campanile* is in danger. The Ponte Vecchio may still collapse, and half the goldsmiths on the old bridge have lost everything in the flood.

The former Consul-General and his wife have been to the American consulate, two doors away from us, and met an Italian friend there, the director of Fratelli Alinari, the huge print shop whose gutted interior we saw this morning. The director had come in desperation to ask for advice. Since the shop stands on that part of the river front where the retaining walls crumbled, the buildings there took the brunt of the flood's attack; the river rushed into the shop with such force that it tore a marble fireplace out of the wall and swept tables and counters from the front rooms into the back rooms and, circling out again, poured pictures, lamps, decorated boxes, and tables from the rear storerooms into the front. All the records of sales and orders, together with hundreds of packages ready to be mailed to the States for Christmas, were found lying in confusion under mud and water on the floors, addresses washed away, the goods irretrievably damaged, the big ledgers reduced to pulp and illegible. 'What can we do?' the director asked with tears in his eyes. 'How can we let our customers know? What will they think of us? We do not even have their names!' He wanted somehow to get word to America that his firm was not breaking faith with its clients but that the situation here was terrible and he did not know how to reach them.

We all feel numbed, our mind haunted by images of the bleak scenes we have walked through and of the suffering on the faces we have seen. There is no real news; everything we hear is still rumour, and we feel shut away from the truth as well as from the world outside. Though the waters have drained away, Florence is isolated by a flooded countryside. A few amphibious army vehicles have reached the city, but nothing is going out, not even mail or telegrams. The post offices are flooded and the telegraph wires are down.

The sun sets in a clear sky and tints the blackened city with soft pink light, and nothing moves in silent Florence except the hushed pedestrians and the rescue crews of the Misericordia and the firemen.

Sunday, November 6

Morning dawns clear, and the sky is pale, wide, and open. The day is like a Perugino painting, the small objects in the foreground picked out against infinite pallid space, so that the chief effect of every scene is emptiness. A Sunday calm can be felt in the air, but it smacks of hollowness rather than of Sabbath peace. The number of persons on foot, walking toward the centre to stare at the ravaged streets and the blackened buildings, is far larger than yesterday; but these people also are silent; even their footsteps are muted by the mud through which they carefully tread.

In the cold early light we find a newspaper spread on the desk in the downstairs hall – an extra with red headlines got out yesterday at Bologna by *Il Resto del Carlino* for Florence's *La Nazione*, whose immense new rotary presses, the pride of the town, are sunk under water and clogged with mud and grit.

FIRENZE INVASA DALLE ACQUE

La città trasformata in un lago

the headlines read, and our bright-faced, competent blonde friend says gratefully, 'We can read at least *that* much Italian, thank heaven. I swear that I'll never travel again without learning the language.'

But as we search the pages for specific news, we find almost none. The reporters obviously had as little detailed information and were as much in the dark as we have been. The paper reports that there was a flood of similar severity in Florence in A.D. 1270. But of further news there is only confirmation of what we already know: Florence is isolated and is without light, food, and water; the roads out of the city are still muddy torrents, and aid sent from nearby towns has been unable to reach its destination because the highways are broken and awash.

The professor and his wife and I decide to walk to the railway station, to see whether a paper may not have come out today, for the lack of any news but rumours increases the feeling of solitude in which we live and makes the isolation of the town seem more threatening than it did even in the hours of violent emergency when the waters surrounded us. We take the long way up the Lungarnos, to avoid the impassable Frato, which is still a lake, turning inland at Ponte alla Carraia, and wading and sliding through heavy mud on a roundabout route.

Some corners are still blocked by mud and water too deep to wade, and the streets look even more cluttered than they did yesterday, so that it is startling to discover the Piazza della

Stazione half cleared of major debris. Crews of labourers are at work piling up the trash, and a garbage truck is moving slowly along the open space south of the station, while at its gaping rear doors two men with shovels are steadily though not very rapidly scooping up whatever amount of litter a shovel can cope with.

How can they possibly hope to cart away all this junk in garbage trucks, the professor wants to know; it is crazy, it is absurd: the shovels might as well be teaspoons in the face of the mountains of refuse with which the city is heaped high. Still, they have cleared this one small space. Such hopeless doggedness makes us want to cry. They are heroic, these obstinate Florentines, and so is their patient use of whatever limited means are at hand against this overwhelming debacle, when even Hercules would hardly be any good faced with what these slowly toiling city employees are contending with.

Pumps are chugging away at the entrances to the underpass, though these are still choked by trees and battered automobiles; and lines of water from the flooded depths streak the mud that covers the paving stones of the square. We pass the entry to the huge underground garage, which holds two hundred cars and is full of black water to sidewalk level, and are made sharply aware of the reek of gasoline. A big hand-lettered sign warns: *Pericolo di fumare!*

The vast empty station contains two little crowds, one at a news-stand and one at a *tabaccheria*, where cigarettes are going fast, and at pre-flood prices we are gratified to learn; there is no inflation. We are able, after a wait, to buy today's *Nazione* (printed at Bologna) before the supply is exhausted. The banner headlines read:

FIRENZE DEVASTATA DALL'ARNO
vive con calma ore tragiche

The lead story praises the 'exceptional gifts of calm and courage of the Tuscan people,' and we look at one another and spontaneously exclaim, 'How right they are, how right they are!' 'I'm so glad that somebody is saying so.' For it is this calm control that covers heartbreak and ruin that has made this beleaguered and battered Florence even dearer to us than she was in the days of safety and prosperity. Only an occasional outburst of anguish, which dies after a few words, only the eyes of the people reveal the pain that underlies the calm that has marked them during these three bitter days. The paper calls the disaster a cloudburst and reports only thirteen dead all over Italy in the general storm.

The desperate situation of the people who live in the houses in these narrow side streets is becoming cruelly apparent. Every basement stands full of water, and it was the poorest families who lived in cellars and ground-floor rooms. The ground floors contain little besides mud, and along the sidewalks there is a growing accumulation of splintered chairs and tables and of thin old mattresses that have blotted up the oil and are sopping with flood water. Most of the poor who were flooded out have lost all they ever owned, and many have left only the damp garments in which they are dressed.

Food is coming into the worst sections from relatives who live above the flood line, and there are many greedy hands waiting to receive it, but there is not a great deal, for Florentines do not keep a stored larder but buy every day's supplies fresh at the morning's market, and the great central markets are still under water and nothing is coming in from the buried countryside. Bread is being distributed by the firemen, for the bakers of Fiesole have been up all night baking bread for the empty stomachs of the *alluvionati* on the flats below. It is not enough, but the promptness and warmth with which it is offered brings cheer to the voices, and there is much anxious shouting when a little help arrives. In the districts where the water still lies deep in the streets, the firemen pole their boats along the house fronts, and baskets on cords are lowered from upstairs windows and carefully drawn up again with a precious burden of loaves and a bottle of mineral water or a flask of wine.

Threading its way through the mangled square where the medieval bulk of Santa Maria Novella rises, a line of women appears, carrying handfuls of candles, the tall white votive tapers that worshippers light before the statue of a Madonna or a favourite saint when they make a special prayer. One woman holds ten of them to her breast. Remembering that the dark comes on at four thirty and that candles are scarce at home, we wind our way around blockades of damaged cars to the littered open where the graceful façade of the church has looked down on six centuries of Florentine drama, and after retreating once before the overlapping flats of muck that have buried the wide steps, we find a little track that can be waded and enter the open door on the left.

A Dominican priest in white-and-black robes is unrolling a new bundle of tapers at a small table just inside, and he serenely offers us all we want to buy at a hundred lire apiece. We hesitate to take too many, and finally we each buy six, a dollar's worth. The interior of the church is black, and though we strain our eyes we cannot see the striped Gothic arches of the nave or even make a guess about the damage. We try to remember how high the Masaccio fresco of the Trinity stands from the floor along the left aisle, because the height of the oil streaks on the doors makes us fearful.

Even more frightening are the open entrances to the chapels low on our right as we come out again, for they are below street level, and the interiors, the Green Cloister, the Spanish Chapel with its elaborate frescoes, have been flooded full and are still oozing oil, the walls covered with what looks like a ten-foot-high blanket of molasses. There are pools of water on the floors. We gaze at the desolation around us.

It is hopeless, we say to each other, the town is lost. They'll never, never be able to recover from this. And we feel a distress that is physical and lies within our stomachs like a lump of indigestible food.

Everything looks hopeless today, the debris, the aimless small efforts of the people at work, the lack of organization, the size and monstrous extent of the ruination.

On Ognissanti near the river there are five-foot-deep caverns in the pavement which extend for half a block. An antiquary's shop looms empty, while before it on the narrow sidewalk a collection of collapsed eighteenth-century chairs and gilded tables, their wood bleached and cracked and most of the colouring lost, their rose-and-gold brocades rotten with oil, tells a piteous story of loss. I stop to stare with my mouth open. A boy in boots and an apron is carrying out buckets of sludge and dumping their contents into the deep ditch of the street, while a grey-haired man in a respectable Sunday overcoat stands in the street across the cavern and calls to him, *'Carlo, Carlo, là in giù.'* The man turns to look at me, and at the sight of the pain in my face, his own face becomes distorted and he seizes me by both forearms, bringing his eyes near to mine.

'Terribile,' I say miserably. He throws back his head and takes a harsh gasp of air.

'Trent' anni di lavoro,' he says in a smothered voice, *'in cinque minuti – scomparso.'* Then he drops my arms and turns his attention to the boy. *'Carlo, la scopa.'*

In the grey light of late afternoon in the *salotto* we pore over the papers and share news that we have gathered in the town. We learn that by seven o'clock on Friday morning, when we were first gazing in shock at the river, the flood was already in the streets at the Ponte Vecchio; the whole centre was swamped before ten. Thousands of Florentines are without roofs or houses; there are stories of last-minute rescues from basements or from second stories by perilous ventures in a small boat over the swift current. There is a rising toll of deaths, of people who hesitated too long before trying to flee toward safety, men trapped in stalled cars and drowned, invalids and old people who died in the beds from which they were helpless to rise. The staff of the *Nazione*, coming down into the square after an isolated night above their drowned presses, found the arm of a man protruding from the mud.

All normal life is at a standstill in the city, and the emergency is increasing rather than diminishing. In poor sections and in the countryside there are still people marooned on rooftops, waiting for rescue, while the walls of the houses crumble and the roofs begin to sag. In some places high wires and TV antennae make rescue by helicopter impossible; one touch of the wires and the helicopter would be lost. Rumour tells of two old peasant women on a roof who did not know how to buckle the rescue harness and who slipped from the sling as they were being drawn up to the hovering helicopter and were dashed to death. (It turns out later to have been one old woman, but it happened, and the wonder is that rumour kept the count down to two.)

There is a first staggering tally of the art treasures that have been spoiled or lost and a plea from the directors of art for immediate aid to save paintings and manuscripts. Only the beginning is known as yet. The Medici Chapel is flooded, the cloisters at Santissima Annunziata cannot be entered, the Bardini Museum with its fabulous collection of ancient musical instruments may be beyond saving. The worst are only mentioned; no one knows anything so far – the cloisters at Santa Croce, the vast underground stacks of the National Library facing the Arno, the Buonarroti house where Michelangelo's drawings are. The city archives going back to antiquity lie underground and cannot be reached for the water. The illuminated manuscripts in the

Cathedral Museum are sunk under a layer of soupy mud. Help is called for, and hurry, hurry. Much may be saved if aid comes fast enough and there is money.

We hear of the heroic struggle by the directors and a handful of staff members of the Uffizi who breasted the climbing flood to reach the galleries, some of them striving for two hours to cross the torrents in the streets, and who laboured without rest or food for a long day and night to save masterpieces from lower floors and from restorers' laboratories where the waters were already piling in. Among many others, a Masaccio and a Filippo Lippi were carried above the flood, and a massive Giotto, too heavy to carry, was hoisted above the water by pushing it up on to a scaffolding, where the flood just lapped its edges. Professor Procacci, superintendent of galleries, rather than let his staff take the risk, hazarded his own life to rescue the hundreds of priceless portraits that lined the walls of the corridor running from the Uffizi to the Pitti Palace above the quaking Ponte Vecchio. Dr. Baldini, in charge of restorations, and Dr. Becherucci, the woman head of the Uffizi Galleries, performed prodigies of salvage and also risked their necks. Then in the light of morning of the fifth, when the water had gone down, they stood and cried for what they had not been able to accomplish, for works in the underground laboratories where the flood burst in before help could arrive, for the treasures they could not reach. The Florentines do not feel that the wealth of art of their city belongs to them alone, but that they are custodians of a priceless heritage that belongs to the whole Western world.

'We do not cry like children,' Giorgio Batini wrote in his story of the lost art in the *Nazione*, 'but like men accustomed to struggle and now bowed down by too vast a catastrophe, by a disaster for which words fail?'

At supper we eat potatoes, with a little ham that Dario has miraculously conjured up from somewhere, and we are grateful to be eating at all. In the house we wash in a pint of cold water from the bathtub reserves, and we use the toilets like chamber pots; the boys flush them twice a day with a bucket.

'The one saving grace in this ghastly mess,' the professor says bitterly, 'is that there aren't any TV cameras grinding, there aren't any reporters going around with microphones. Imagine the obscenity of one of those brash boys going up to some poor dazed little shopkeeper, with all his worldly goods lying in a muddy pulp on the side-walk, and saying breezily, "Now how did *you* feel when this happened?"'

When the dark arrives, I fix two of my new candles into the necks of mineral-water bottles and put them in front of the mirror on my dressing-table, so that the reflected light from the glass will be bright enough to let me see the keys of my typewriter. I can read the pages only when I carry them into the direct glow, and then I have to squint to make them out. I begin to understand how Milton went blind. When my fingers grow stiff with cold, I warm them by holding them around the little flames.

CHAPTER THREE

Fango

Monday, November 7

The morning is crisp, and in the cold air the daze that follows after shock is beginning to clear from our minds. Life is stirring again, but what is still here is the mud, the *fango*.

There are other Italian words for mud: *melma*, which means slime, and *mota*, which means sludge or mire, and we use these too, for we have all of them; but it is *fango* in which we tread, *fango* in which we sink ankle deep, *fango* with which our boots are thick and our clothes spotted. The city is a quagmire of *fango*.

There has been hardly a start made at getting the mud removed from the buildings and shops and houses, there is so much mud, there seems to be nothing but mud. Now that the water is seeping out of it, the mud comes out of doors in heavy blobs that bend little shovels and that the brooms have trouble dealing with; and as it comes out, the long barrows of slimy debris in the streets mount higher and higher and block the way from kerb to kerb, wherever you turn, whatever street you try to make your way through.

Except for the thousands of private hands still patiently and unweariedly at work, there seem to be almost no efforts to clean up or clear away. Everything lies where it falls or is thrown – in the choked streets. The *comune*, we are told, has only one excavating machine.

The one sign of community enterprise is the pumps, at work here and there removing water from cellars, for underground Florence is still a lake. But the city has only a hundred and fifty pumps for an area of nearly a square mile crowded tight with buildings in a city of over half a million people, and it takes a day to pump out one small basement. And the first efforts to get rid of the underground water must be made at all hazards in the great public buildings where invaluable books and documents lie submerged and disintegrating. The National Library on the broken water-front, whose priceless and irreplaceable collections of rare books and manuscripts rest in the vast stacks below street level, was one of the first to be cleared of water, and now only an acre of *fango* remains.

Everywhere the *fango* is slick with fuel oil which, we learned today, came from the heating plants in the big buildings, which exploded as the flood swept in, and whose heavy fuel spread this pervading scum which covered the tide and then the city. In all the narrow streets the mud is starting to stink of rotting refuse, spoiled foodstuffs, and sewage. It gets inside shoes, leaks into galoshes, spots stockings; and it can't be got off by washing in a pint of cold water, especially when we can't buy soap. But last night, through incredible luck, the cold led me to open a trunk to get out a comforter for my bed and on the very top, wrapped in plastic, lay my snow boots, which I has forgotten I had with me. I can wade in them through depths of muck where I could not walk before.

So I wade, and in many streets the pumps are grinding away, flushing out the cellars, and in every other block it is possible, in the streams from the hoses, to wash off the globs of mud that make my feet heavy – a cleansing that lasts for about fifteen feet. But these streams are being used for more vital matters than cleaning boots.

At every outlet stands a group of women and boys with buckets, wash-tubs, copper jugs, and many with only a collection of wine flasks in a net bag, waiting to carry away the precious flood water to wash floors with, to soften the mud, to wash walls, to wash the few objects that remain whole and look as if they can be saved, to wash until the precious water itself becomes thick as mud and has to be thrown out.

In every street there is a small procession of people carrying water, and in every imaginable sort of container. They smile in recognition as they pass each other, and one group of five laden with wine flasks begins to joke about the size of their containers as I follow them. *Coraggio*, things are looking up.

And today water is coming into town in trucks. In the square at San Lorenzo a big red truck bears a sign: ACQUA – NON POTABILE. This is simply scrubbing water, and there is a queue of nearly fifty persons with jugs and cooking pots and bottles, all looking unreasonably cheerful. I understand that drinking water is also being distributed, but I have not seen any trucks with drinkable water.

The danger of an epidemic in this stinking and waterless town has been on all our minds. This morning the first health news appears. Building corners and arcades are plastered with posters carrying a *proclama* from the board of health. Boil all water, the posters demand in large type. All containers for water must be boiled; foodstuffs and particularly vegetables must be carefully washed in sterile water and thoroughly cooked in sterile water. These warnings have already gone out on the radio.

There is no typhoid or epidemic, the signs announce, but the danger is latent. Butcher shops and fruit and vegetable markets are potential sources of infection, and the first efforts will be made to clear them. Absolute collaboration is demanded of all citizens to report any animal carcasses to the provincial veterinary office without delay. Army trucks will carry them away.

Near the Ponte Vecchio the mud is a deep soup and the stench is a miasma. But laughing in the foul air, two American girl students greet me, full of a new enthusiasm. They are high-booted and wear gloves and raincoats. They are off to the Palazzo Pitti, where there has been a call for help to start the first steps of restoration for the works of art that are being carried to safety there, still coated with mud from the restorers' shops and other flooded buildings. 'It's wonderful to be given something to do,' one girl says, and the other looks down at the cluster of curled leather wallets in the mire of the street and says thoughtfully, 'How fragile *things* are.'

The whole town is a testament to the perishability of things. But the great Renaissance palaces of hand-chiselled grey or golden stone stand solid and enduring, though a twentieth-century catastrophe has begrimed their feet and dirtied their faces; and just now the people of Florence are beginning to look as imperishable as their buildings.

Coming home to my typewriter after only two hours in the city, I find that the first telegrams are getting through; I have a wire from a friend in Rome who was to join me in Florence on Saturday, the day following the disaster: FLOODS BROUGHT CANCELLATION TRIP TODAY CIT HOPES GET THROUGH SUNDAY TOMORROW WILL COME DIRECTLY TO PENSIONE PLEASE ADJUST RESERVATIONS. Sunday was yesterday. Of course I hadn't expected her. But what could the people in Rome have been thinking of, I ask myself, to let her make plans to reach here?

There is a police cordon around Florence tonight to prevent looters from entering the town; it is also a net stretched to catch escaped prisoners from the jails, for about eighty of them, released from their cells to save them from drowning, got away over the roofs.

The sunset over Bellosguardo and the Arno is a wash of pure flame, the famous *tramonto rosso Fiorentino*, and a faint haze lies over the towers and palaces and bridges, softening their outlines before night buries the lightless city in blackness again.

Tuesday, November 8

The morning is icy, with fog shrouding the hills, but within two hours a pale sun shimmers over the cold city. The guests here have spent the past two days trying to dry out their cars in the muddy courtyard and get the engines running. They are leaving as fast as they can get away. The first train for Rome left last night, the lobby is full of suitcases, and by this afternoon there will be only seven of us left in the *pensione*.

In the street at the back soldiers gather around little fires at the kerbs, but they don't seem to be doing anything but searching the trash for bits of wood to burn. The seeming lack of organization is disturbing, and no one knows what the officials are accomplishing, though there must be emergency jobs of frightening magnitude to be handled.

Today again, it is private individuals who are toiling away at the same old tasks; they have taken their survival into their own hands – at whatever cost in energy and misery and discomfort. The lack of aid from outside the city has turned many faces bitter – we are being ignored and neglected – but it has only hardened the people's determination. It has also strengthened their disdain for the government; for Florentines are stout individualists and have always distrusted bureaucracy. In this crisis there is no help to be hoped for; they must do it all for themselves

There are few spots to walk in on the sidewalks, and the streets are impossible barriers of debris. On to these endless and mounting trash heaps have been tossed all the perishable stuff of daily living and interchange, all the life that was, the discard of the commerce of Florence and the contents of her homes – scattered over and filling higher the burial mounds of mud that jam the streets and fill every narrow alley. Two crates of shattered ice-cream cones, slabs of chocolate, wrapped candies thrown out in the street and filthy with *fango*; masses of soaked cardboard and matted wrapping paper, cartons and rags and wet rolls of gummed tape and broken boxes of bond paper curled and brown – I have never seen so much paper and cardboard, now all steeped in oil and dirty water and mixed with gravel.

In the wide market of San Lorenzo where the emptied stalls are being scraped and scrubbed with unclean water, the rubbish lies in heaps fifty feet long and six feet high. Within the mud are matted apples and lemons, paving stones, dented suitcases and vanity cases, sweaters, wine flasks, work shoes, gloves, antique maps streaked and torn, straw bags, cracked souvenir ash trays and statuettes; and at one end dangle filthy strings of black, green, and red chiffon lingerie trimmed with cheap lace – lost, one imagines, to a somewhat dubious clientele. On some piles the litter can't be distinguished from the mud that covers it. On the paving near the stalls the mud is scattered liberally with buttons of all shapes and sizes – a little milky way of shining bits of bone, glass, and metal.

A priest in his robes strides along the gummy way, carrying two pairs of red rubber boots over his shoulder. A woman in a fur coat steps gingerly from one thin spot to another, holding a Pekingese in her arms above the muck. There are no children in the streets. Shabby men poke here and there at the edges of the trash heaps and now and then stoop to pick up some chipped and useless little object. The stall owners watch them angrily.

High and white with sunlight at the corner of the square, Giovanni delle Bande Nere in marble sits on his pedestal. The sun is warm on the red domes of San Lorenzo, but the big doors of the Medici Chapels are wrenched off their hinges and bent inward, and oil streaks them for six feet above the street.

In Via Giglio the mud heaps are spangled with shells of Christmas – tree balls, red and gold and silver and blue, and long strings of greasy tinsel loop through the rubbish. A dozen sticky dolls lie on top of one mound, and an old woman in black picks one of them up and wipes its face with the corner of her apron, upon which the shopkeeper runs out from the doorway and snatches the doll from her, scolding her furiously.

'*Per mia nipote,*' the old woman whines.

'*Si può pulire!*' (it can be cleaned) the shopkeeper shouts, and the doll goes back on the rubbish heap.

Alas, how many pieces of spoiled merchandise are being set aside in the sorry hope that they may be made clean again and saleable. Washers, electric stoves, electric irons, TV sets that have been soaked in mud and *nafta* for four days and nights are lugged out to the hoses from the pumps and washed clean of their outer coating of filth; but what has happened to their inner mechanisms I don't even want to imagine. This sort of forlorn hopefulness seems more tragic than outright loss.

In Piazza Santa Maria Novella in the street before a shop that sells kitchen furniture, a brave refurbishing is going on.

Clean gas stoves and shining white kitchen cabinets stand on the paving stones where the mud has been scraped away a little. A stout woman with a bucket and stained rag is washing away at a half-cleaned cabinet, and as she wrings and rinses and polishes, she is singing. Her voice is pleasant, and she sings several bars of a popular street song about *amore* (they are always about *amore*). I cannot help it, I am so caught up with admiration for her that I call out, '*Brava!*' and she answers with a wide wave of her arms and a frank smile. '*Bisogna cantare,*' she calls back to me, and as I watch her she goes back to work and goes right on singing. I don't have to be told what she means: *Bisogna cantare per non piangere* – you have to sing to keep from crying. But she makes no show about it, and I think, this is what courage is, when you get down to it. These people will survive because they refuse to pity themselves.

At the National Library on the torn water-front, where the destruction is appalling, the river border washed away and the mud in huge banks obscuring the entrance to the building and burying the turned-over cars, students are gathering. They have been here since yesterday, from all parts of the town, boys clean-shaven and trim or long haired and bearded, girls in the high boots that are fashionable this year and now are proving strictly utilitarian, many of the girls in blue jeans, even Italian girls who ordinarily would never dream of wearing anything resembling trousers in public. They are Italian students from the university, young Americans from three Florentine study groups and many from courses at the Accademia or simply here studying on their own, English students, French students, students from all over Europe – hundreds of them are coming as volunteers to the library and to the galleries to offer willing hands and strong young backs to a labour that could never be accomplished without them.

In the dank and stinking underground stacks of the Biblioteca they began by scooping out the slimy mire in bucket chains, sweeping, clearing a path. Now they have formed a long line stretching from the lower depths all the way up the stairs to the higher floors where it is clean – a chain of three or four hundred young people (at takes that many, the distances are so long), working in an atmosphere so poisonous that they have to be supplied with gas masks, standing ankle deep in sludge and passing from hand to hand, hour after hour, the pasty blobs of mud that are rare books and manuscripts. On the upper floors the books are wheeled away and ranged in endless ranks, bindings up, and sprinkled with sawdust or talcum in a first attempt to get them dry enough to begin the slow work of cleaning and interpagination – when restoration is possible.

They are already a closely united crew, these students. Their attitude appears independent and off-hand, but they are devoted, because there is a job to be done that means something for a change. On the higher stairs, where the air is breathable, a song starts somewhere along the line, usually an Italian song, and is carried by untuneful but vigorous voices up into the open.

Nothing is so heartening to the town as the sudden springing up of this volunteer corps of students. Casual and joking and singing and working like dogs, they are the first solid and trustworthy and uncomplaining helpers to arrive – in the face of the baffling unconcern and indifference of the world outside our gates – and they come from within the city itself, like the shopkeepers, a second home-bred relief crew going ahead at full steam with an obstinate optimism that ignores obstacles. And their uniform is mud. Their faces are streaked, their clothes plastered and caked from heels to shoulders and dappled with oil stains that will never come off. The townspeople out of their own scanty stores begin to bring them food and wine, to invite them home for a meal, to provide snacks and cigarettes during the work breaks, when they all go out on to the steps in the open air for a chance to breathe and a few minutes of letting down.

I speak to one American girl whom I know, a hot-eyed little girl with black hair, who is so ardent that she scorns these moments of relaxation. 'Just a bunch of bums,' she spits out. 'Look at them there doing nothing.' The boys laugh at her, but they finish their cigarettes before they go back to the job.

There are two wires waiting for me at the *pensione*, one from friends in Paris offering me refuge, the second from my friend in Rome saying that the CIT bus lines will bring her to Florence on Monday. Today is Tuesday. For the first time today we are being allowed to send wires out of Florence, so I plod over to the station, where a crowd of people is waiting outside the telegraph office in the dusk. But a generator is grinding, and there are lights inside, and I stand in line for an hour among the pushing crowd, with much help from two brisk young Italian girls ahead of me, who aren't going to see me lose my place in line, and finally I am able to push two telegraph forms under the grille. The wire to Rome is accepted, but the wire to Paris is thrust back at me and refused. 'Why?' I want to know, but I can't hear through the glass with the crowd chattering around me, and I have to bend my ear down to the crack below the grille.

'*Qui solo in Italia*,' the clerk shouts at me; any wires out of Italy have to go through the central post office. But this is too much. I have walked so far today, and it is cold and dark, and I *can't* labour through these bogs again all the way to the central post office, to stand in line for another hour or two. There is no help for it now. Only the one wire will get off.

I make my way home through the cluttered streets, and near the station the streetlights are on, though there are no lights in the houses. In the dark streets off at a distance the *carabinieri* carry torches. The way grows increasingly dim; there are no streetlights along the Arno.

(It will be Friday before I receive a reply from my friend in Rome and learn that she was actually in Florence yesterday. 'What a relief to get your telegram,' she wrote. 'I had asked the Red Cross to hunt for you.' The bus from Rome set out at seven-thirty Monday morning with eight passengers, a girl hostess, and the driver and his helper and, after a tourist stopover at Assisi, took a roundabout way to Florence hunting for safe roads. From the outskirts of the city it took two hours to reach the bus station, and meanwhile dusk had fallen.

'How we got through I still don't know,' she wrote, 'and I am still positively sick at some of the sights we saw. The watermark on some buildings was eighteen feet high. When we reached the bus office they had accommodation for all eight of us at a *pensione* with no food, no water, etc. We, of course, went. There was no electricity, and one saw the ruin of floors and the watermark of eighteen inches. We went to a store across the road and bought packaged cookies and bottles of water. I tried to telephone you, but your line was broken. There were no taxis; I asked the hotel man how to walk to you, but he was horrified and said it would be absolutely unsafe for me to try to walk to hunt you. Anyway he was sure the Pensione Consigli was evacuated because of its location. CIT should not have taken us from Rome. We were the first bus to go and the people just didn't realize conditions. They took us back to Rome at eight the next morning, all just heartsick at what we saw ... but I shall never forget the faces of the people, sobered and determined. I haven't been able to relax and have had the joy of my trip dampened.')

*

Back at home in the candle-lit *salotto* the few of us who are left, huddled in our winter coats, talk over the mounting tale of damage. The losses at Santa Croce and its cloisters now seem to be terrible, and the great crucifix of Cimabue, one of the prime landmarks in the turn from Byzantine to Renaissance art, waits for immediate attention and may be irreparably lost. Rescue crews may be able to enter some churches tomorrow. A hundred paintings are known to be gone, and three or four hundred more are damaged, no one knows how badly, among them a Lorenzo di Michelino, a Bicci di Lorenzo, a Neri di Bicci. The soaked frescoes are blistering. A Botticelli and a Tiepolo are now known to be among the works saved, by heroic efforts, at the Uffizi during the flood.

But it is the life of the city that is in crisis – everything paralysed. Half the industry of Florence is destroyed (a correct estimate, it turns out), all the artisans flooded out, and tools, materials, and finished handwork vanished or demolished. The industrial workers are scattered, their places of employment gone, many of them without a roof over their heads in this cold. Neighbouring towns are still inundated, farms stripped, fields and vineyards and gardens buried under mud flats, cattle drowned by the thousands. Cars are still stranded in water on some highways. The city itself lies buried deep under mud – cold, dark, hungry, and forsaken. We haven't even seen a Red Cross car

It seems so hopeless. '*Ora povera Firenze,*' our little Signora says in a shaking voice. *Povera Firenze!*

Tonight the bland voice of the Rome radio announces that 'Florence is returning to normal.' – '*alla normalità.*'

Wednesday, November 9

'*What* normality?' the *Nazione* demands in a blistering front-page editorial designed to shake up the sluggish government bureaux at Rome, where an uninformed complacency seems to take it for granted that since the waters have subsided Florence has no problems. Rome has been calmly announcing 'normality' at Florence for two days now, and an influx of cars of friends and relatives who have been led to believe the trouble over has created a vast traffic jam around the edges of the impenetrable town and hindered the arrival of relief vehicles.

Piero Bargellini, the conscientious mayor of Florence, whose own house was heavily flooded, has just issued a desperate appeal to the government and to the cities of Italy to send earth-moving machines to remove the deep blanket of mud and detritus under which the city lies buried. Bulldozers, scrapers, dump trucks are needed at once if Florence is to survive. Two battalions of army engineers are labouring at cleaning out the worst areas, but they don't have proper tools, anymore than the people have.

'How is it possible to remove this liquid mass with hand shovels?' the Mayor pleads in a frantic attempt to be heard by some official ear that will listen.

The food and drinking-water situation is easing somewhat. People wait their turn patiently at the food distribution centres. Flooded grocery stores are opening on city orders, but packaged goods, flour, and pastas are all soaked and lost, and the harried shopkeepers stand with a rag in hand to wipe the worst of the oil and mud off of cans and bottles rooted out from the jumble on the floors, most of the cans without labels and identifiable only by guess as belonging to the shelves near which they are found, the bottles recognizable by their caps once the mud is scraped away. I buy a sticky can of tomato juice, which turns out to be pineapple juice once I get it home and cleared and opened, but any sort of fruit juice is a boon with our diet of potatoes and spaghetti.

This is the fifth day since the deluge. The sky is cloudy and the air bitterly cold; it is too cold to rain. Ambulance sirens howl all day long.

Still, for the first time, there are signs of stir, of something getting done. Two Red Cross stations are open, and a contingent of nurses is coming in today from Rome. Along the upper Lungarno appear lines of American Army trucks, loaded with food and water, and dump trucks filled with American soldiers are moving toward the endless heaps of waste.

Vaccination centres are open and hundreds of persons are queueing for typhoid shots. The city is distributing three kinds of chlorine to safeguard drinking water. Electric generators have been found for the hospitals in the central areas the patients still crowded on upper floors where the valiant nurses and doctors carried them as the flood burst in; and new patients are constantly arriving – parturient women desperate for medical attention, the injured, old men and women suffering from exposure.

And first aid for the art of Florence is pouring in. Restorers are arriving from all over Italy; monks who are experts in the restoration of illuminated manuscripts have flocked in from their monasteries. Art experts are flying in from abroad, from America, from England. A generator has been supplied for the recovery rooms at the Pitti so that the rescued paintings may dry at an even temperature and not crack and buckle hopelessly before the hands of the restorers can reach them. Yet even today, after five days, the paintings in the Church of Santissimi Apostoli cannot be reached by the rescue crews.

This morning for the first time I manage to penetrate the blocked narrow streets of the Santa Croce district, and everything I have seen till now pales before the sights here, in these thirteenth-century streets as constricted as alleys, winding among houses of the same vintage where the poor inhabit dark and heatless rooms. These streets, so near the first overflow of the river, took much the worst of it. Fuel oil blackens every house where the water raced through for twelve hours, fifteen feet high, and oil is a thick crust over the liquid mud through which my boots squelch and slip and in which rotting garbage is thick and sewage stench is choking. Every peeling old building is gutted and damaged, walls cracked and doors and grilles torn out, windowsills crumbled, the narrow rooms resembling sewers, the mud and putrid matter inside a foot deep. The demolition is incredible. Bulging house walls are roughly shored up with poles and timbers. Some sections are blocked off and crude signs warn of falling cornices – *pericolo* – for the flood has so softened the soil that supports these ancient houses that their foundations are sinking and many stand empty in danger of collapse. I have never seen anything so black and void as these sorry streets – it is like dug-out Pompeii.

Before I reach Santa Croce Square I am very nearly struck by a block of falling cornice, a solid lump of brick and centuries-old plaster, which crashes down about three feet in front of me and shatters into powdery fragments. It is not exactly prudent to walk here, yet there are men here at work.

Piazza Santa Croce is devastated. It is covered by vast mud flats, and the stairs of the great Franciscan church are so overlaid with overlapping quilts of mud that the boots of the men who have climbed them have left deep depressions – like dinosaurs' tracks, I say to myself, for the horrid scene leads to extravagant similes. There are wrecked cars and a heavy accumulation of trees and tree trunks, and a number of soldiers are toiling away with shovels at the edges of the waste. The church cannot be entered, but there are soldiers inside pushing at the mud with shovels and wooden scrapers. The oil lines on the walls and doors of the church show all too plainly what must have gone on inside. This is one of the finest and largest of the churches of Florence, dating from 1294 and containing priceless frescoes by Giotto, by Agnolo and Taddeo Gaddi, and by Giovanni da Milano, which cover vast areas of wall space in transepts and chapels. Along the walls of the aisles within the church are ranged the handsome marble tombs of the most famous of the sons of Florence, Michelangelo, Galileo, Machiavelli and the cenotaph of Dante, who died in exile from the Florence he both loved and reviled and whose tomb is at Ravenna. Santa Croce is called the Westminster Abbey of Florence, and there are writers, musicians, and statesmen among those awarded a burial place here. Set into the floors are blocks of medieval burial slabs, many of them carved with marble effigies of ancient Franciscan prelates and Christian knights in armour. The church is warm in tone and handsomely proportioned, and the variegated lights from its slender stained-glass windows give it a cheerful air which reflects the spirit of its gay and gentle saint of the birds and animals, who spoke of the sun as his brother and water as his sister.

The last time I was in Santa Croce before the flood it was evening, and the lights of the candles for the mass brought a rosy reflection from the frescoes upon the lighted space, while the huge nave receded into twilight dimness and a choir of voices chanted the 'Canticle of the Creatures'. Now water and *fango* and *nafta* have taken it, and its paintings are stained and its marble saturated with brown fuel oil, its altars befouled.

*

Tonight there is a quiet little party given by the former Consul-General and his wife, who will leave for Nice in the morning but will be back in Florence for Christmas. That will leave five of us at the *pensione*.

CHAPTER FOUR
Soccorsi a Firenze

Friday, November 11

This is the eighth day since the flood and the weather is very cold. I wake to the rumble of heavy motors on the Lungarno outside my windows, and for the first time since Bargellini's appeal, the first time in these dragging days a continuous line of large trucks is moving into town along this main avenue. The big truck bodies are loaded with tractors, scrapers, cranes, pumps; and now and then with a clanking of heavy cleats huge bulldozers clump along in the procession. There are long lines of dump trucks, most of them carrying extra equipment. My heart is suddenly light. I have never seen a more beautiful sight that this sudden generous inpouring of aid for the desperate town. It has taken long enough, heaven knows, but help is here at last.

This used to be a one-way avenue leading toward the centre, but all traffic laws are in abeyance to permit the use of any street clear enough to let cars through, and against this tide of trucks there presses a far thinner line of tow trucks dragging *alluvionate* cars out toward the edges of town. Things are finally starting to move. Some of these cars have sprung hoods and boots and dented tops; some are whole but painted brown with *nafta*, the windows inside and out as brown as the bodies, the interiors upholstered with caked mud.

There are other signs of progress. Silvana, the pretty maid, when she brings in my breakfast tray, has a surprise for me. Smiling, she goes to the washbasin and turns the tap, and there is an abrupt snorting gush of brown water from the pipes. '*Non potabile, non si usa,*' she warns me. The water is unsafe for anything but scrubbing, and we are forbidden even to wash our hands in it, but we can flush the toilets – and what a luxury that is! There is a big pitcher of hot spring water for a sponge bath and a small pitcher of spring water for drinking and brushing our teeth. We have been brushing our teeth in mineral water before this. Every little civilized advance is a surprise and a pleasure these days and quite beyond our expectations.

Dario, the ever resourceful, has finally dried out his small car and got it going, and at five in the morning he was chugging off to the hills with the back seat full of big clean cans to fill with fresh water from a *sorgente* at the Piazzale Michelangelo. He went even farther, to the hill farms, and has returned with fresh eggs, vegetables, ducks, and chickens. We shall eat magnificently again, though he has managed omelets and meat before today.

After breakfast the last three transient guests depart, their car finally repaired and in running order. One of these is our bright-faced friend whose competence and cheerfulness have encouraged us all through these grim days, and who spent yesterday helping Dario and the boys wash off wine bottles rescued from the cellar. All three who have hung on so long are reluctant to leave; the troubles we have shared have created a tie among us. They hug the Signora, we all exchange farewells, and with much waving and many calls of '*auguri*' and '*arrivederci*' they are off for Rome. The Signora and I come back into the echoing lobby. All around us the big handsome rooms of the house stand empty; where there were twenty guests a week ago, now only the Contessa, who has not considered departure, and I remain.

'But now there are only two of us left!' I say in wonderment to the Signora, and she suddenly embraces me, laughing shakily, and then with a burst of mirth she exclaims, 'No, no, there are three. There is the Contessa's personal maid.' We break into a simultaneous fit of laughter. Nevertheless, these will be hard days for the house, without clients, as they will be hard days for all the enterprises of the city, which have been brought to a full stop.

With the big earthmovers ploughing their way along like teams of elephants, by late afternoon many of the streets in the heart of town are already nearly cleared of tree trunks, car bodies, high mounds of mud, and major refuse. It is only right to have begun here where the life of Florence centres, and the clearance brings the people a new breath of optimism, though there are miles and miles of blocked streets and alleys which it will take weeks to clean out. Even in the cleared streets at the centre the mud and water are still thick, and the kerbs are bordered by a five-inch-deep mire. Near the Ponte Vecchio you wade through a real swamp in the street, a malodorous mud that is wet and soupy. '*Peggio della guerra*,' a man mutters who is slopping through it, but he doesn't really look disgruntled. If it hadn't been so much worse than this before, the filth and destruction would still look impossible; it is the arrival of help that has brightened the face of our small world.

Everywhere in this part of town the big scoops and blades are lifting and shoving. Dump trucks move out in file, piled high with loads of heavy mud, paving stones, branches, rubbish from shops and houses. The trucks bear black and white signs on their cabs: COMUNE DI RIMINI – SOCCORSO A FIRENZE; COMUNE DI FORLI – SOCCORSI A FIRENZE (Forli itself was flooded); MILANO – SOCCORSO A FIRENZE. One after another the Italian cities are responding. There are snow scrapers sent by the highway departments from the mountains to the north; some of the heavy equipment has come from as far away as Switzerland and Germany.

The firemen of Florence have been performing prodigies, working often around the clock from the day of the flood itself, saving lives, carrying aid, transporting the sick; and so have the men of the Misericordia. Now two major sources of potential infection, the fish market and the meat market, have been cleared by firemen who went in in gas masks to shovel out in putrid masses the fish and flesh which, when they came in fresh, were designed to feed half a million people.

All over town there is a stir of hope. A teenage boy goes by me, singing cheerfully in the street. Brooms and shovels are still swinging on every hand, and the people look just as determined as in the first cruel days, but a little less desperate. They shrug and say, '*Pazienza*'. They smile.

The old Florentine spirit of mockery is reviving, and stories about the flood, most of them authentic and touched by a new tone of light irony, are beginning to make the rounds. There was the man standing on the Ponte Vecchio on the morning after who observed thoughtfully, 'It's a good thing the Arno isn't the Mississippi; we'd all have drowned.'

There is the shop owner who hung out a sign on the boarded-up front of his ruined place: 'I have had to close my shop because I am nervous.' The city government is the butt of a good deal of mockery. The only thing that survived the flood, people say, is the town council at city hall; it was the only thing light enough to float.

There is the story (Mayor Bargellini told this one himself) of the man who woke at seven on the morning of November 4 in his apartment near the Ponte Vecchio and looked down from his window to see the flood streaming through the street below. 'I know that Bargellini promised to clean Florence,' he muttered, 'but I think this is carrying it a little too far?'

I carry these tales home to cheer my friend the Contessa, whose face and gentle voice are so full of distress over the ruin of the city that I have not had the heart to tell her the worst of what I have seen.

For the essential misery grows sharper with the passing days. There are six thousand families homeless; there are thousands of workers without employment, the machinery destroyed in the factories where they worked and the goods ready for consignment totally lost; it will take months, perhaps years, for restoration. Meanwhile these people stand empty-handed and without prospects amidst the wreckage and plead for public assistance.

A friend who acts as agent for artisans' shops and secures orders from America for their products tells me that all his artisans have been flooded out and he has no idea when work can begin again. Day after day he visits their mud-filled shelters, where the cleaning goes on all too slowly. Their hands are stiff with cold; the daylight goes at four and without electricity no one can work at night. Their tools are gone, Christmas is near, there is little hope of their getting Christmas orders ready on time, and even if by unbelievable strain they manage to fill some of them, the chances are overwhelming that the orders will have been cancelled and the goods will be left without a market. His artisans are not complaining, he assures me, even though time enough has passed for them to begin to count their losses and understand how little is left them.

Nobody is complaining. A profound sentiment has spontaneously sprung up among these people that they bear a common loss and are embarked upon a common prodigious effort to survive and to remake their lives; thus to plead a special grievance would be to set oneself outside the pale, just as to ask any special privilege would seem wrong to them and shocking; they are all in this together.

The city too is beginning to count its major losses. Six thousand out of the ten thousand shops of Florence have been wiped out. Ten thousand cars were caught in the centre and damaged or demolished. The number of works of art injured or lost has now reached thirteen hundred, and there is no hope for the Cimabue crucifix. Millions of books lie under the mud.

The University of Florence, pulling itself out of the muck, has found nine of its ten faculties gravely damaged and its libraries lost. The university has always been poor; now it finds its lighting and heating plants destroyed, scientific and architectural equipment ruined, the chemistry laboratories completely gone. The loss is estimated at two billion lire. Here too the students are toiling away to lift the libraries out from under layers of mud and water, but the cost of restoring the books will be beyond counting. Eleven thousand students can hope for no classes to begin before January.

The worst losses to public monuments have been suffered by the ancient Palazzo di Parte Guelfa, the Church of San Firenze, the convent of the Badia, and the house of Dante. But Michelangelo's beautiful tomb groups in the Medici Chapel are unharmed, praise be; and though the Carmine was flooded, its Capella Brancacci, which holds the frescoes of Masaccio and Filippino, remained above the waters. The incomparable vast galleries of the Uffizi and the Pitti Palace are, of course, on the top floors and were not threatened. The losses at Santa Croce, however, are frightening; the enormous flood that swept into the church and invaded the cloisters whirled like a turbine and rose in an agitated lake that filled the cloister to the very capitals of its pillars and soaked and battered many of the great art treasures of the town. The lovely Quattrocento intarsias are falling apart; the whole scene in the ravaged church and cloisters is chaotic.

When I stopped by the American consulate this afternoon, an old Italian, his hands large-knuckled and calloused by labour and his face twisted with anxiety, came in and began reciting a plaintive litany of his experiences: his house was swept clean of possessions – mattresses, furniture, clothing all smashed or swept away. His daughter and little granddaughter, he thanked the good God, were safe, but what would come now? How could he feed them and take care of them? 'Who will hire me now, when there is no one left who can even afford to hire a clerk?' he asked. '*Destituzione,*' he said coldly, '*destituzione.*' He is a gardener,' the secretary told me simply.

Sunday, November 13

By yesterday afternoon the worst debris was gone from a large part of the centre, though of course the mud is still everywhere. It was wonderful to see the streets unencumbered. As soon as a street was cleared, the cars began coming in, though only authorized cars are allowed in that part of town. Every windshield carried an official paper, which must cut down the driver's vision considerably, and the labels read *servizio assistenza* or *medico* or *autorizzato*.

I walked down Via Calimala to look for the watchmaker's where I had left a watch to be cleaned – not to ask him for it, God forbid, but just to tell him that if it was gone it was gone and not to worry about it; but the shop was boarded up, and it looked as if no work was being done there. There were still brooms and shovels everywhere, and what came out of the doors was lumpy and thick. But here and there the first signs of recovery were appearing. Two doors away from my watchmaker's, two shops were open, one dress shop and one shop of fine linens, and there was nothing shoddy or makeshift about the opening. The windows would have graced the Florence of the old days, the glass gleaming, the walls inside fresh and white, knitted suits and scarfs in shades of rose and blue on display, and a cut-work linen tablecloth extending its elegant invitation to buy to any customer who might pass by. Inside, the polished floors were covered with sawdust against the mud that we all track around, the few shelves were freshly painted, but the merchandise was pitifully scanty. Most of the shelves were bare.

In a little side street I found a *fruttivendolo* in business again, and I bought lemons from Sicily for my morning tea.

A few of the washed-out shops contain rickety tables at which piles of *merce alluvionata* are being sold for pennies. Here the floors are dirty, and the curious finger more than they buy. There are miserable leather bags, key cases, cigarette cases, and wallets, blotched, stiff from the water and badly wrinkled, mud in the cracks when you try to open them. There are garments that have been plucked out of the mud and water and dried, a few only spotted, most of them in bad shape. A number of these shops display hand-lettered signs, most of them ironic: 'Direct from the mud to the consumer! These fabrics have been pre-soaked and are guaranteed not to shrink.' In Borgo Ognissanti, which is still a bog obstructed by mountains of debris, these little tables stand out on the dirty sidewalk in front of two or three of the dark and empty shops – and there is nothing worth buying, though the poor are gathered there turning over the heaps of stuff judiciously, little girls' dresses, muddy sweaters, ruined leather, and bolts of damp and dirty yard goods. Merchants from the floating stalls at the Straw Market are offering mats and hats and baskets, all limp, dirty, and much the worse for water. Nothing, I conclude, looks sadder than drowned straw.

But there are bargains in some places, where good merchandise has come through in much better condition. One of my student friends came to see me yesterday afternoon, wearing a handsome coat she had bought at an *alluvionato* price and which had had only a little mud along the hem. She had also bought a fine leather bag, whose stained exterior she thought she could clean up, to send to her sister at home for a Christmas present and a souvenir of Florence and the *diluvio*. 'When I looked inside I gave up, though,' she said sadly. 'I could just see my father take one look and yell, "Typhoid!" and throw it in the fire. I'll keep it for myself, I think.'

She had just come from the Teatro Comunale, the opera house of Florence, which stands across the street behind this little palace and which was so ruinously inundated that the whole orchestra floor was destroyed, the seats rooted up and scattered, stage, scenery, and costume rooms washed out, stage machinery and switchboards and heating plant a confusion of metal and wires. The girl had gone to offer her services in the work of restoration and had been refused. The interior was 'still too dangerous' for volunteers to enter, she was told.

Out in the air on this bright Sunday, the big sight is the procession of laden dump trucks climbing the ramps of the Ponte Amerigo Vespucci, where soldiers have removed a long section of railing and where the big truck bodies slowly tilt and spill their massive accumulation of refuse into the river! This is the answer to the question of where all the mud and debris can go. The town is giving it back to the Arno, which brought it in.

Somehow it doesn't seem a very thoughtful solution to the problem. Already the stones and mud are creating banks around the piers of the bridge, and the whole span is trailing with a fringe of rags and straw that hangs down nearly to the surface of the water. The river is too low to carry away easily what it brought in, in spate; and if the dumping obstructs the riverbed, there will be new problems when the next period of high water arrives. It seems typically Italian, however, this happy-go-lucky choice of a means at hand to get rid of the waste, this decision to 'do what we can now and worry about the results later'. Mechanical efficiency is not one of the outstanding endowments of these people; if you call in a plumber to repair a broken tap, he is likely to study it for ten minutes and then announce, as if he has made a discovery, that 'it doesn't work'. Technical effectiveness is not only lacking, it is out of character in a people whose concern is with the graces of living, with ease and good manners, with honour and dignity, and with family life – old-fashioned virtues perhaps but strongly rooted here. In the great industrial city of Milan to the north, where modern efficiency has caught on and sets the tone of living, the pace is hectic, faces look harried and impatient, voices are sharp, and one sadly misses the grace and courtesy of the Tuscan people, whom the Milanese scorn for their backwardness. Between these two extremes, there is much to be said for patience and graciousness and inefficiency – and Florence. (As it turns out, by nightfall on this Sunday the engineers have already seen the danger and have moved to control the dumping into the Arno.)

Below the bridge, where the sandbanks now stretch out toward the riverbed and the stream runs shallow again, for it has been dropping steadily, incredible masses of this discarded refuse have come to rest on the banks. For a quarter of a mile the sand is almost invisible under tumbled piles of wood: slats, beams, broken boards, endless webs of splinters, and shattered crates, chairs, beds, and tables. Scattered among the fragments of wood lie black mattresses and torn blankets, rags and shoes and purses in shocking profusion, and above all, paper, paper, paper of so many hues that the coloured trash looks like the spread of confetti on the streets in carnival week. From a distance it looks almost gay in the winking sunlight, but from close at hand it is a sickening refuse heap of the city's substance, and through this litter rise the stripped spines of the trees and bushes of the riverbank, dead, black with oil, and supporting on their denuded branches rough balls of rags and straw, caught out of the current, so that it looks as if colonies of untidy herons had nested there. Climbing over this waste wander a dozen ragged scavengers, poking among the litter, but it is obvious that even they are finding nothing worth the picking up, except for one man who is gathering drenched sticks for firewood.

The Sunday parade on the Lungarno is larger than ever, and the faces look tired but patient. Today there are children in the crowd. The people shake their heads at the sight of the cumbered riverbanks, and fathers lift little boys on to the parapet to give them a look or let them walk along the wide cement top, gripping them firmly by an arm. Almost in front of our doors a growing group of people has halted to look over the wall with concerned and fascinated faces.

A large swan stands down there on a patch of bare sand. It is a magnificent bird of unusual size, its back and wings shining white, but its breast thickly covered with black fuel oil. As we watch, it curves its graceful neck and with its beak makes an impatient swipe at the coating of oil on its feathers; and then it goes into a state of anguish as the poisonous stuff fills its nostrils; it writhes its neck up and down, opening its beak wide, and finally rises up on its webs with its huge wings outstretched until it stands as tall as a man. Its tail lifts, and a spurt of black droppings hits the sand, where there is already an accumulation which indicates that the great bird has been there for some time. There are no web tracks on the sand, and it does not move except for this abrupt, tormented flinging out of wings and throat. Now it subsides again and the wings fold, but the neck still tosses, and then the swan turns its head and beats its beak against a wing, trying to wipe off the filthy gum that adheres to it. It saws away for almost five minutes before it appears to have found relief; then it shudders and tucks its head under the wing and crouches low and still, its feet out of sight.

'*È morto*,' the newcomers say, peering over the wall to see the bird, but the others assure them that it is not yet dead.

After about ten minutes the lovely neck lifts again, and the swan gazes about it, weaving its head from side to side. Then again it makes a sudden stab with its beak at its befouled breast and goes through the same wing-flapping agony of suffocation, and again it rubs its beak over and over on its wing feathers, shoots out a little stream of black excrement, and at last shrinks into a deflated ball with its head out of sight.

The surface of the river, I observe, is still coated with oil, as it has been for the past nine days. The swan is obviously very sick and will undoubtedly die if it is not caught and cleaned. As the big bird huddles motionless, the crowd of watchers thins out, and now three of the people from the *pensione* come hurrying across the street, our little Signora carrying pieces of bread to toss down to the swan. But the swan is not interested in eating.

'*Povera bestia*,' the Signora cries in distress, wringing her hands.

'Can't we do something?' I want to know, and she is as eager as I am to find some help for the superb creature, which is stirring again and starting to repeat its wretched struggle to get rid of its burden. We go back to the house, and the Signora tries to telephone the society for the protection of animals, but there is no answer. 'It is Sunday,' the Signora says; 'they will not be open. Besides, the society was *lagata*.'

'Why not call the police [the *questura*]?' I ask. But at this suggestion the faces of the Florentines change and turn withdrawn. To call the police is obviously something that isn't done, not for the sake of a swan. But suddenly the Signora flashes with enthusiasm again. 'You could call the police.' she says eagerly. '*Per un' Americana non fa la brutta figura telefonare la questura.*' She hunts out the number and rings it and puts the telephone into my hand. I pull myself together and call up the best Italian I am capable of, and in a moment a deep male voice answers in the most musical accents I have heard for some time, the pure Florentine, in which this beautiful language is at its clearest and most flowing.

'I am an American living in Florence,' I begin speaking. 'There is a swan of the Arno on the riverbank below the Ponte Amerigo Vespucci, its breast covered with *nafta*. It tries to clean itself with its beak and the *nafta* chokes it. The poor creature doesn't know what to do ...'

'*Un cigno dell' Arno?*' the grave voice repeats after me, with such sympathetic concern that my heart turns lighter and I manage to tell all the sorry story in detail. 'It will surely die if there is no help,' I conclude, pleading; and the beautiful concerned voice repeats carefully all I have told it and asks specific questions about where the swan is to be found. assures me; 'something will be done,' and he thanks me earnestly and courteously for having let him know.

Everyone in the house is full of delight, and the Signora and I embrace in pleasure and relief. But twilight is coming on, and the big ball of white feathers on the sand is not moving any longer. Night falls, and there has been no sign of a rescue party. But in the morning the swan is gone.

(It is a week later when the Signora seeks me out, her eyes shining. Three of the great swans of the Arno have been saved from the *diluvio*, a news story has announced. Two were found far down river, their breasts coated with *nafta*, and one was recovered near the Ponte Amerigo Vespucci last Sunday when '*una cittadina*' called in and reported its presence. 'You are the *cittadina*,' the Signora says, her face alight with satisfaction, and I am as happy as she and feel singularly honoured by the title.)

CHAPTER FIVE
Si Ricomincia

Tuesday, November 15

The weather is very cold, and the town lies under a high, dark fog, through which the pale sun breaks now and then, only to disappear after five minutes, behind the murk. Soldiers with rifles stand at all the street corners. The Lungarno is crowded with scrapers and dump trucks in procession, as aid continues to flow in.

The centre is free of encumbrance and two-thirds of the streets have been cleared of the worst debris, but as the refuse goes and the pumps empty the flood water from the cellars, a new trouble is showing its head. The cellars are loaded with mud, which is now beginning to come up out of them into the streets. On all sides booted men are carrying up buckets of mud-thick water, a heavy slop from below street level, which accumulates along the kerbs in a new layer of muck mixed with gravel and crumbled plaster and smelling of sour fermentation and mould. Mingled with the mud, spoiled supplies that were stored below and all the worthless trash that collects in cellars, together with the furniture of families that lived in those dark rooms *sottosuolo*, are coming up into the open, and the mud is topped by this profuse discard. It is beginning all over again; the streets that have been scraped will have to be cleared a second time; there seems to be no end of it. Soggy, blackened mattresses appear unventilated basements hazardous, and a number of the workers who are cleaning out below ground, firemen and soldiers among them, have been overcome by poisonous *nafta* fumes and have been taken to hospitals.

For the first time, today I see signs of reconstruction, not just of getting rid of the flood's leavings. On the cleared Lungarno between Ponte Santa Trinta and Ponte alla Carraia the street is quite clean; it is possible to see the old brick-and-rubble construction of the river walls where the pavement is gone in deep cavities near the parapet that was; and stacks of heavy corrugated metal forms lie along the street and near the bridges, looking strangely shining and new. Where the Lungarno disappeared near the Ponte Vecchio, big trucks of the Lavori di Pronto Intervento are spilling loads of rough stone to make a fill, though there are few workmen here as yet, those on hand being occupied with clearing and unloading. At noon the workmen build hot little fires on the mud-free sidewalks to heat their coffee pots, and they eat leaning against long sections of new water pipe that wait for installation. Farther along the Lungarno crews are at work unblocking and flushing out the ancient sewers.

At the Palazzo Strozzi, where the National Institute for Renaissance Studies and Art History is housed, long files of students line the stairs. engaged in the rescue of books. The great Vieusseux Library is coming up out of the basements, some volumes soaked, some lumps of mud, all moving up hand to hand to the dry upper stories, where two whole floors are already covered almost solid with books ranged cover to cover and coated with sawdust. Sawdust is thick on the stairs and on all the floors. These are handsome young people in spite of their muddy boots and gloves and garments; some of their faces are intense, some are relaxed and amused, and the books move up the double file in a rhythm to which they keep time by singing. The Florentines in gratitude have nicknamed this priceless army of youthful volunteers the '*angeli del fango*', and they are immediately recognizable on the streets, not only by their youth and their long strides, but because they are muddier than anybody else and their faces are so confident. They wear their mud as a badge of honour, and nobody had better suggest their cleaning it off. Nineteen-year-old Clare from a university in Minnesota, a tall, candid-faced girl with long dark hair, reacted vigorously when another girl started to scrape at the mud spots crusted on her skirt. 'Leave those alone,' Clare protested; 'they're my souvenirs of Florence. I'm going to cover them all with plastic and they're never going to come off.'

This big golden Palazzo Strozzi now houses the offices of the International Committee to Rescue Italian Art, for which large contributions and small are flowing in daily, a generous rush of aid that has revived assurance in the battered city and fortified the courage of the thousands who are labouring to save her heritage of beauty. The world has not forgotten Florence. Men and women and children and institutions in circles that stretch across oceans have felt a blow at the news that this precious city has almost been lost to the world, and their response has been swift and heartening. The Florentines no longer feel alone and ignored. Long lists of new gifts are published every day, and the work is moving, though there is almost too much to be handled and it must be handled at once to ward off major losses.

The first week of rescue work for the art was complete confusion, and all the help was volunteer, with hundreds of students arriving at dawn to help lift paintings, statuary, film records, manuscripts out of the slime and carry them to emergency refuges for the first steps in drying and cleaning. Now the first funds of the Committee to Rescue Italian Art (CRIA) are going for a crash programme to save the frescoes, for these are in greatest danger, the *nafta* still an inch thick on the Uccellos of the Chiostro Verde at Santa Maria Novella, the Botticelli and the Ghirlandaio in the Church of Ognissanti damaged – I watch four young men at work there cautiously cleaning the lower portions of the beautiful 'St. Augustine' and 'St. Jerome'. It is the wet in the walls that is the greatest threat, for earth and foundations are drenched and the water is rising in the walls and loosening the colours. All the marvellous frescoes in the choir at Santa Croce are in peril, for though the flood lapped just below Giotto's scenes of the life of St. Francis, the water seeping up through the walls is pressing salts out to the surface, and the salts are physically pushing off the paint. Elsewhere, statuary, illuminated manuscripts, tapestries and paintings wait for hands enough and funds enough to rush them on their way to rescue. In the long run, the art experts believe, it may take twenty years for all the restoration to be accomplished.

Warm clothing for the dispossessed and homeless is pouring in by planeloads from America to the consulate and is going straight to the people as fast as it comes in. Where they can, the Florentines too have been quick to share their own clothing with the ones who were left with none, for there were many families who woke up to find the water already knee deep inside their houses and who escaped in their night clothes, without even being able to find their shoes. The *Nazione*, the city's responsible and well-edited newspaper, has been collecting its own *fondo di benificenza* and has been putting ready money in generous sums into the hands of families who are in most desperate straits, stripped of all possessions, homeless and penniless and shivering. The Anglo-American Committee, in which the American and British consulates have joined forces, is doing the same thing with gifts of funds from abroad and, with the help of churches and of the San Vincenziano, the best of the local volunteer relief groups, is handing out money as well as coats and trousers, dresses and sweaters to these unfortunate *alluvionati*.

Thousands of families who were flooded out of their homes and who are housed in barracks and cold schoolhouses are pleading for houses or apartments to live in, and there is nowhere for them to go. Popular-housing developments and fourth-class *pensioni* have already been requisitioned, but with over half the city flooded (and the most populous half) and their former homes wet, insanitary, without light or water, and many of them in danger of collapse, there is just no place to put these sorry people. A little cash in hand is what they most desperately need, for wages from regular jobs and from the shops just aren't coming in anymore. And all those valiant broom-and-shovel people are contending with want as well as with the burden of cleaning out so that they may live again, and they still don't know what they are going to live on. The city has 18,000 families on its relief rolls and is giving all the aid it can.

The more I see of the destruction all around us, the more I marvel that our slight elevation along the river preserved this little *palazzo-pensione* from complete disaster. In the Cascine, the area of wide parks that lies just down river from us on the other side of Ponte della Vittoria, the river swept straight over its banks, and great cracks are opening in the earth there and the riverbank has caved in. The carcasses of a hundred and twenty drowned racehorses that were housed there in the racetrack stables have been dragged into a long line and attacked with flame throwers. They turned out to be too waterlogged to burn, and they have finally been tumbled into a dug pit and covered with earth.

Army trucks have carried away the bodies of the camel and the small animals that perished at the Piccolo Zoo, which used to be a favourite haunt of children and lay below the race-track. There is no zoo left now, for the full sweep of the river flowed straight in across the whole low-lying Cascine and rose above the tops of the wire enclosures. Stags, does, and wild hogs in their terror leaped out or broke out and fled to the woods above, but goats, monkeys, peacocks and hawks, hedgehogs and other small creatures drowned inside their protective wire nettings.

At the *pensione*, two young American girls travelling in Italy, who stumbled in here yesterday, left this morning, full of shock and distress. I visited them last night in their room, where they were packing by candlelight, and their healthy young faces were round-eyed and stricken.

'We came because we heard there had been a flood and we thought it would be interesting,' they said with troubled voices. 'We had no idea – we never imagined it would be like this; it's so awful! Nobody outside has any idea of what it's like in Florence. You can't believe it; you couldn't ever believe it if you didn't see it. We got scared when we first arrived, and it got worse when we walked, so we went to the American Express. And when we saw the American Express! well, then we knew we'd better get out fast.' The American Express offices stand in the square at Ponte Santa Trinita, and they resemble a huge echoing barn, darkly stained and wet, with only one little counter remaining far at the back, where business is being carried on by the light of small candles set in saucers.

Wednesday, November 16

This afternoon the lights came on here in the house, to our common rejoicing, though many districts are still dark and there are no streetlights on the Lungarno. For days now the Signora and Dario have been promising me an electric stove for my room when the electricity was restored, and they brought one in at once – they have bought big ones for me and the Contessa. But alas, the current in the rooms isn't strong enough to take them; so they were carried out again and small heaters substituted. My room has not been especially uncomfortable, it gets the sun all day when there is sun, but I had forgotten the pleasure of sitting before the glow of an electric fire, which feels completely luxurious. Civilized comforts are very nice when you can have them. It troubles me, however, that the *padroni* will continue to do without heat themselves.

I was down to the last pair of my sixteen votive tapers (I had gone back to Santa Maria Novella for ten more), and when I turned on my desk lamp, I was so used to dimness and candlelight that the brightness of the electric bulb nearly blinded me.

There is news today of serious importance to Florence: there is to be an inquiry into the causes of the unprecedented overflow of the Arno on the tragic fourth of November. Four times in over six centuries of her history, the city has been invaded by destructive flood waters, but only the great flood of 1333 can be compared with this year's catastrophe. The last flood came on November 3 and 4 in 1844, and the marble markers on Santa Croce that record the high water of that year are two metres below the oil streaks left by the overflowing river this sad November. And this year two great hydroelectric dams, constructed only twelve years ago up in the high hills of the Valdarno, should have protected the city in the valley bottom against excessive high waters. Now Rome has appointed a commission of Florentine judges to investigate the massive release of water at the dams at Levane and La Penna on the night of the third, for though the rain in the preceding twenty-four hours amounted to almost a third of a year's normal rainfall, and though there were lesser floods all over Northern Italy on the fourth, the startling speed with which the waters rose here – three feet in an hour at one point – the speed at which they ran, and their abrupt subsidence have raised doubts about the proper control of the sluices at the dams. There is conflicting testimony about the amount of water impounded on the days before the flood, about a failure to lower the level of the reservoirs during the heavy rains; and there is strangely divergent testimony about the hour at which the flood gates were thrown wide. There is also disturbing evidence that the records at the dams for that crucial night have been altered. Among the people here there is a slow burn of anger and a sharp demand for knowledge of what went on.

Evening brings letters from home and from friends in Europe, many posted some time ago, for the mails have been slow and the post offices must still be in a tangle. Most mailboxes along the streets are taped shut, since their interiors are full of mud and water. My mail is curiously mixed; some letters contain frantic appeals for news, some are almost ludicrously unconcerned. Family letters are full of advice not to run any risks; friends in Chicago who have seen television pictures of the flood beg for word of my safety; there is a letter written two days after the flood from a friend in Ohio who trusts that I am out of boots and back in proper heels again. A boy who was a student of mine two years ago at a Pennsylvania college and who is studying in England on a shoestring has sent a dollar and a ten-shilling note for some family I may know that has been flooded out. Three Peace Corps boys in Africa have scraped together twelve dollars and sent it for flood relief. A girl in New York hopes the 'bad weather' in Italy has not inconvenienced me.

Saturday, November 19

The sight of the town is still one of such bleak devastation that it makes me sick to walk in it, but the people are so wonderful that they fill me with pride that human beings can behave like this. 'How is it that they aren't broken down by losing simply everything and by the burdens they are carrying?' I ask our little Signora. 'You'd think they would be hopelessly tired after two long weeks of cold and back-breaking work when the progress in mopping up is so slow and now there is all this new mud. But there are no tears, no complaining, just a shrug and a smile, and they are hard at it for another day.'

She says gravely, '*Piangere adesso vorrebbe dire finito*'. To cry now would mean we were finished.

We still slop through *fango*, and it is thick in many places, especially heavy around Santa Croce, where the bogs of mire have a bad smell and where whole rows of unstable house fronts have now been shored up by long timbers. In Borgo Santissimi Apostoli, just a block from the Ponte Vecchio, the teetering front of the house of the Amidei plot is supported by a framework of heavy beams, and the narrow street is a pond, where it isn't choked with debris, and is too deep and treacherous to be waded.

Outside the opera house at the back, the red velvet carpet that used to cover the orchestra floor lies in great loops and folds of muddy stuff along the sidewalk. In front of the big underground garage at the station, a tractor in the street is snaking out at the end of a chain the cars that have been soaking for fifteen days in mud, water, and *nafta*. They stand streaming with water and all of them are plastered brown with oil. Earth-movers are at work in the streets out from the centre, in spite of the fact that many of these giants are being recalled for snow removal in the mountains. Only a block from the station a huge Caterpillar Traxcavator and an International Payloader are scooping up mud, debris, and trees and spilling them into a dump truck.

In all the radiating streets, once the huge mounds of waste have been carted away, you see people out in the street washing things. Protected by raincoats, overalls, or aprons and using buckets and rags or hoses and scrub brushes, they scour away with good will at shelves, sections of counters, cracked chairs, whatever has been saved that may be able to be put to use again. There is a great deal of badinage among them. Behind them their houses and shops stand hollow and oil blackened, windows gone, doors broken, in many of them even the lighting fixtures ripped from the walls. But how the people polish and how patiently they clean! Their faces are quiet and rather gentle. None of them talk about courage or put on a look of courage:

their quietness is courage. It is impossible to restore their city, and they are restoring their city. They are patient, but it is the patience of untiring labour, and Italians are not afraid of labour.

'You must be dead tired,' I say to a tall, lean peasant woman of fifty. I know her, and I have been watching her heaving out into the street a tub of water that would strain the shoulders of a man.

'Who would make a fuss for a little hard work? It has to be done, so we do it,' she replies, giving me a broad smile, but her eyes betray kindly amusement at my American softness and inexperience. 'You know, my family, we are *contadini*,' she goes on, resting her hands on her hips, 'and I grew up on a *podere* near Fiesole. From the time I was five years old, my sister and I used to go down every morning a quarter of a mile to the spring with big copper jugs like that one (she indicates a foot-high jug a neighbour woman is using) to bring back water to the house, for drinking. It was heavy, but we didn't mind, because it was *bello* to be out in the air in the morning where everything was green. You get used very quick to carrying.' She shrugs. '*O sí, nell'inverno* hands and feet got cold; we were always barefoot. But what I like is to remember all the green, and looking down into the valley where the olive trees looked like fog, they are so grey.'

Still, the mud is everywhere, and the oil sticks like glue. There are no detergents, since detergents dissolve rapidly and of course didn't survive. There is only water and the muscles of tired backs and arms, and each new-polished counter is a spot of brightness in a landscape of pervading filth.

In Borgo Ognissanti the walking is still risky. Mud in great lapping soft cakes lies along the kerbs and over half the street, blocking the sewer slits. The stench of the mud and gravel being flung out from cellars is oppressive. Here too the shops stand void and stained. But near the corner, on the door of a narrow shop, a *tabaccheria*, a sheet of paper pinned to the entrance reads in bold red crayon:

APERTO – SI RICOMINCIA

The brave little sign fills me with such admiration that I go inside and buy a pack of cigarettes that I don't particularly want. The interior is completely refurbished, though there is only one small counter, with a few shelves behind it at the rear on the wall. The walls have been painted white, and the handsome young proprietor points out to me the line to which the water came; and there it is, unquestionably, five inches below the thirteen-foot ceiling, a broad streak of grey showing through the new paint where the oil would not come off. The centres of two shelves hold small supplies of cigarettes and tobacco, and that is all there is for sale. The young man's face is almost stupid with pleasure on this day of reopening, and I shake hands with him heartily and wish him *molti auguri*. His expression softens to wonderment.

'To me it is a *meraviglia*,' he says softly. 'I didn't dream, I never dreamed that it would be possible?'

No other shops show any remote sign of being ready to open, but two blocks farther up, on the Prato a fair-sized stationery store on the corner displays a narrow strip of tablet paper reading APERTO, and needing paper, I enter at once.

Shelves and counter are whole here, and at the counter two women, one old, one young, are cleaning muddy ballpoint pens, taking them apart, cleansing them meticulously, and rubbing them bright. A man is labouring in the back, clearing out mounds of matted paper, mushy and brown. The ceiling is fifteen feet high here, and only on the two top shelves is there any merchandise left; all the way down the long damp walls the rest of the shelves are empty. The man comes out cheerfully and with the aid of a ladder manages to find a ream of rather cheap paper for me on one of those high shelves. The losses, they tell me, have been *'terribile'*. They carried fire insurance but had not thought of flood insurance. Nor had anybody else in Florence.

'Ora bisogna molta molta pazienza,' they say to me, smiling at me but with strain showing in their eyes. *'Molta pazienza.'*

Today there is a report on the health of the population, which is good. There has not been a single case of typhoid – and all credit must go to the mayor and the health officers, whose immediate and heroic precautions have warded off this all-too-real threat. Tetanus shots and vaccination against typhoid are still being urged, and orders to boil all water, to use disinfectants, and to wash all food are plastered everywhere.

The final count of the dead is posted: in the province one hundred and twenty-one dead, six missing; in Florence thirty-three dead, though rumour persists in citing a higher figure.

Engineers have been called in to clear the mass of debris out of the Arno.

Monday, November 21

Today as I walk, I make a discovery: even on the back streets the mud is thinner than it was a week ago. When you tramp through it every day, you don't observe these gradual changes, until one day they strike you as a surprise. The people have been steadily sweeping and hosing off the sidewalks, which are no longer blocked by great lumps of mud but wear a thin slime, in some places not even an inch thick; but as the mud becomes thinner it grows more slippery, for my feet keep slithering and it is hard to keep my balance. This lighter look is not true of the quarters that took the worst flood damage, however. Around Santa Croce and in Gavinana the blocked streets look like shell craters, and they haven't even begun to be dug out.

There are new signs of progress. The government in Rome has moved at last and has passed a decree providing funds for public works here, for restoring hospitals and schools, for housing the state archives, for the repair or rebuilding of factories, for loans to artisans with a postponement of interest payments. Subsidies are provided for flooded farmers to rebuild demolished barns and dwellings, to sow crops, to provide feed for their animals, though thousands of cows, oxen, pigs, turkeys, have been drowned. (Although the provisions are impressive, everyone knows that there is a bureaucracy to deal with, and weeks later, with thousands of artisans applying for immediate aid, there are only one hundred and fifty printed forms available. An American Chamber of Commerce drive will do much to re-establish the artisans.)

Large Italian business firms are offering free replacements of their products to flooded Florentine shops. The major Italian publishing houses will replace their lists free to bookshops here that have gone under water. Olivetti will replace typewriters, and many other firms, among them electric-appliance manufacturers and watchmakers, will take back ruined goods and supply new. Fiat offers a forty per cent reduction on the price of a new car to replace any *alluvionata* car up to five years old. All this is very generous.

But it is the very small people, the *popolo minuto*, who are suffering losses that make starting up again look hopeless. I learn of two proud old sisters who lived on the earnings of the younger, an artist who, at the age of seventy-five, made and sold dry-point engravings. All her tools are lost together with most of the furniture, and the two old women are living without income in their clammy apartment, the eighty-year-old sister sick from cold and damp. They have not asked for aid.

There is the thirty-year-old woman who made her living by sewing and was going to night school in hopes of finding a better occupation. She has lost her bed, her middle machine, and her schoolbooks. There is the middle-aged dairy farmer whose son worked with him on the the farm, which supported the two families; their cows are drowned, their garden buried; there is no income and nothing to eat. These are only a few that I know of myself, out of thousands living on the thin edge of desperation.

The saving grace is the resilient spirit the people display, the light mockery, the near gaiety, with which they shrug off their losses. They still laugh, though it may be somewhat wryly.

A doctor's wife tells me about the barber with a shop near one of the hospitals, whose home was invaded by six feet of flood water and who, when one of the doctors asked him, 'Did you have much water in your house, Vittorio?' answered blithely, 'Oh, no, it was a small apartment.'

Today another of the ironic signs went up, this one on the front of a small devastated shop on one of the clogged tortuous streets that wind out of Piazza Santa Croce:

Sufferers from rheumatism
the best cure
Mud from the Via dell'Anguillara
Our mud deposits are open – modest prices
Cash at once or we go under a second time

Wednesday, November 24

At the invitation of friends, Clare, the tall, dark-haired American student from Minnesota, still cherishing her mud-splashed skirt, is taking off with me to spend Thanksgiving at Santa Margherita on the northern coast, where I am to have X-rays for a back injury, since it would be impossible to ask any of these harried Florentine doctors to look after a *straniera* who can get away. It is with reluctance that we feel the train pick up speed and see the houses of Florence slip by. We shall come back, we say to receding Florence; she is our beloved city in fair weather or misfortune, and we both acknowledge that we feel guilty about leaving her for a few days, even with the enticement of medical attention, hot baths, and a shampoo.

The train trip is long and roundabout, for there are still no lines open to Pisa. We turn north toward Viareggio, and for some distance we follow the course of the Arno and for the first time begin to grasp something of the extent of the destruction. Barns and farmhouses are reduced to lumps of rubble, haystacks washed away, vineyards torn out or deep under mud flats, two-hundred-year-old olive trees uprooted. As we come nearer the sea, the farms are still lying underwater, a house roof showing and the tips of fruit trees or a thin dark line of fence posts trailing strings of grapevines, the vines that are planted along the boundaries of all Tuscan fields, since every available inch of land is cultivated here. These slender fence lines are all that tell us we are still passing farmland and not sea. The countryside above Florence along the Arno is in even worse condition, a friend tells me who has been there – 'a lunar landscape', roads scoured out, whole groves of ancient olive trees uprooted, tenth- and thirteenth-century villas left with nothing standing but their walls.

Sunday, November 27

Back in Florence! And how welcome the sight of this disfigured city, although the Riviera was clean and blooming, the sun warm, the winds soft from the sea. Stepping into a tub of hot water seemed like something out of another life, and I feel considerably less smelly and my hair is clean. Yet in spite of the pleasure of being able to relax after weeks in the mud, in spite of blue seas and gardens and orange trees hanging full of fruit, in spite of new acquaintances and the close affection of friends, the life there seemed too easy-going; we missed painfully the courage and strength of Florence, the bubbling, wry good spirits that rise over the enduring pain.

Everyone was courteous and eager to hear about Florence, but the trouble was that you couldn't tell them, it seemed so remote to them, they hadn't seen it. One evening the Richard Burton film appeared on television and gave our friends their first look at the tragedy they had only read about, and they were shocked and almost unbelieving. Clare and I could turn to each other and assure them, 'Yes, it was like that; only there's so much it doesn't show.'

O lovely Florence! odorous and broken and *fangosa*, we are happy to be with you again. Today Mayor Bargellini with a fleet of eight trucks left town to bring *soccorsi* from Firenze to the flooded small towns nearby where help has not poured in as it has here.

Tonight is the first gala night the city has seen since the disaster – the opera is opening. How they have done it in twenty-three days, I can't conceive, but done it they have, and there is music in the city once more. In the Teatro Communale (the opera house) at the back here, the floors are damp and the seats for the orchestra floor have been rented and carried in from a cinema, and since they were built for a slanting floor they have a very odd tilt to them. The heating plant has been replaced, and the house is warm, but only one basement has been pumped out, and the superintendent, Remigio Pavone, announces, 'We are the only theatre in the world to have our own downstairs swimming pool.'

Far above the floor, on the great stage curtain, there is a four-foot-high water line, and a similar black line curls around the boxes half-way up to the first balcony. The stage is bare except for a framework of boards on which the singers can step up for an aria. There is no scenery, only this slender framework against a plain backdrop. The costumes have been lent by La Scala at Milan. But the performance is splendid, the singers are in good voice, full of vigour and spirit and an enthusiasm that is matched only by the enthusiasm of the audience, for this restoration of her musical life seems a promise of the restoration of all life to the shaken city. The opera is Monteverdi's *L'Incoronazione di Poppea*, and the lovely formal old music in this modern hall is a reminder of the centuries of history, and not only musical history, that are woven into the texture of modern life here. The choral singing is by Florence's own Maggio Musicale chorus and is especially well done and strangely moving. At the end of the piece the audience is on its feet for a standing ovation that simply shakes the air.

Clare is with me; this is the first opera she has seen, and she is glowing with delight. Everything pleases her, the fine voices, the costumes, the triumphant tone of the evening, the shouting audience. But when the first call for an encore begins and deep male voices start rumbling swells like bullfrogs, '*Bis, bis, bis*', a dark growl of sound that swells up until it sends chills down your spine, she turns to me bewildered. 'What's going on? Don't they like it?' she asks, and I remember the first night I heard an opera in Italy and that I felt the same confusion until I grasped the fact that this low roaring chant was full-throated masculine applause and a demand for more. The ovation swells and pulses and is full of an exultation that celebrates far more than the evening's performance. Big young men throw their heads back and shout, '*Bravo!*' The applause goes on for over half an hour.

Out in the lobby stands a display of photographs of the wrecked interior of the theatre on November 5, the mud, the pools, the tumbled seats, the damaged machinery. And more immediate mementos are ranged near the doors. Shrunken tailcoats disguised by mud hang on the wall, and below them stand what were once two magnificent Steinways, hardly recognizable, their mahogany bleached white and warped out of shape in six-inch curls, the keyboards an uneven mat of pulp, part sunk, part bulging, here and there an ivory still stuck to the mat at an odd angle. Two harps, twisted, blistered, and colourless, lean toward each other, strings gone or dangling.

Propped against the ruin of one piano stands what looks like a dirty cardboard imitation of the back of a bass viol, and Clare's mouth falls open. 'What *is* it?' she demands. 'It can't be – it is, isn't it?' There is a case full of splinters of what once were cellos, and near it the demolished timpani hoops of twisted brass and wire and crumpled parchment. But gifts to the theatre are arriving already, and on the other side of the lobby there is a new concert grand and a pair of shining bright copper timpani.

Prices will be kept low for the whole opera season, but even so, later audiences will often be scanty, for too many Florentines have lost too much and cannot afford to buy tickets, and there are almost no tourists.

Friday, December 2

It has been pouring with rain again for a day and two nights. The tributaries of the Arno are overflowing and it is running high, though at nothing like its height during the flood. When Silvana comes in to open my shutters in the morning, her grey eyes are full of alarm. '*Ho paura,*' she says, looking out at the river. She is always afraid now when it rains, even during a light shower.

The water is a good ten feet below the arches of the Ponte Vecchio, but the retaining walls are down, and fear of the river now lurks in the minds of the people under all their proud calm. Last night the few goldsmiths who had reopened their shops on the old bridge dashed down in the dark to carry away their goods, and rumour spread that the dams at Levane and La Penna had broken.

The result, around midnight, was a frantic traffic snarl, with hundreds of cars stopped bumper to bumper on the bridges, and the roads leading to the high ground of Fiesole and the Piazzale Michelangelo filled with racing traffic, as people tried to save their possessions and get their cars up to a safe height. Police, *carabinieri*, and firemen have been in a state of alert.

The *Nazione* is very severe with the population because of this panic, which it attributes to an '*allarmismo irresponsabile*,' but we can understand it.

The rain is growing thinner, and life today is back to its old tempo. One good thing the rain has done is to wash a great deal of mud from the streets and sidewalks, and the high water has floated off a good part of the trash that defaced the riverbanks.

There is widespread indignation in the city over a report on Florence that appeared in an American publication. As it has been quoted here it seems another case of *allarmismo irresponsabile* and perhaps a more serious one. The article is said to have reported an immense typhoid epidemic in Florence, over three feet of mud in all the streets, animal carrion floating everywhere, and rats as big as cats both drowned and swimming, the criminals from the jails wilfully turned loose on the town, and the artisans on the point of outright rebellion. These fancies are so shockingly false that my friends among the American students are almost weeping: 'It isn't fair! There wasn't anything remotely like that, and the artisans have been so marvellously patient,' they protest. 'It was bad enough exactly as it was; there's no earthly point in making it worse.'

'It will hurt Florence,' young Deborah says bitterly.

The editors of the *Nazione* treat the report with smooth but barbed courtesy, suggesting that the lady whose 'excess of zeal' produced such details probably meant to help Florence rather than harm but that *'fantasia'* apparently got the better of her. The Mayor of Florence has wired a reply, pointing out that there is no epidemic, not even a single case of infectious disease. 'Many of us do have colds,' he said, 'but these have not hindered the resumption of activity,' and then, suavity deliberately slipped aside, 'The only carrion Florence has are those of her defamers,' and he invited the lady writer who claimed to have been here to visit Florence at Christmas and see for herself.

Wednesday, December 7

The temperature has turned somewhat milder, and the sky is clear blue, the sun striking golden reflections from the stately palace fronts, from which the oil streaks have now largely disappeared, most of them washed off by applying gasoline. There have been great changes in the city in the past ten days, the long labour, the cleaning that had to be done over and over again is finally bearing fruit. It is as if Florence, which had been curled into a tight brown bud, were putting out the first edges of clean and coloured petals. Things have changed for the better. We can even drink the tap water today.

I take a long walk without rubbers down a clean Lungarno, where mud and debris are gone. It is true that in front of one palace near the Grand Hotel there is a heap of basement mud and rubbish big enough to fill two trucks, but one truck is standing by, and there are four men picking up with shovels. The Arno is still brown from the last rain but smooth and slow, with a rainbow skim of oil floating.

At Piazza Goldoni at the mouth of the Ponte alla Carraia, the pavement is clean, though the interior of the big pharmacy at the west end of the square is still a desolate heap of oil-black boards and counters. Borgo Ognissanti is being renewed where it enters the square, and a steam roller is rumbling over hot asphalt, though the sidewalk area is still a pit. Above the square the large metal standing tanks of drinking water wait in the sun, bearing their notices, '*Acqua da bollire per uso potabile*', but there is no one there.

I can walk dryshod along the Lungarno below, where the wall is down, though there are rain puddles in the gaps in the pavement. An elegant old gentleman who is walking here warns me, '*Attenzione!*' and bends down to pull a tile over an open hole in the sidewalk. I thank him and smile, and he grins at me amicably. Here below the old wall, a broad new river wall is going in, built of stones confined in long boxes of heavy wire net. It does not yet reach to either bridge, but there is a big gang of workmen banging away with picks, and trucks are dumping in new stone. Near the Ponte Vecchio this wall is already within five feet of street level.

Everywhere, ringing in the clear air, is the sound of carpenters' hammers and the clanging of hammers on stone. All along the streets lie sacks of cement and piles of sand, tiles, and building stone, while shovels and hods lean against the door jambs. In the empty shops along the river, which are still soaking wet, the walls are being scraped down to the bricks and will have to dry out before they can be replastered. On all sides there is cleaning and polishing. Women and young men and old men greet me with bright faces, in which there is a new light of accomplishment; and they have earned this new cheerfulness, these indomitable Florentines; how bravely they have earned it no one who has not been through these interminable five weeks of struggle and of paralysed civic life can know.

In the sculpture shop below Ponte Trinita, rubber gloves are hanging on the wire grating, and the interior contains headless Venuses, an oil-begrimed Diana, a brown group of centaurs and Lapiths with a tailless horse – all upright once more; there is the screech of a saw far inside and, near the front, a dozen bright statues, while an old man with a tub and cloth is patiently bringing an oily *putto* white. He tells me there is a great deal that they will be able to save. '*Bisogna molta molta pazienza,*' he says, and the words are coming to be a refrain that I hear all over the resurgent city.

In Via Calzaiuoli, a handsome shopping street near the Palazzo Vecchio, all the shops are open and shining as in earlier and happier years; the gleaming glass show windows are full of new leather, silver, embroideries, shoes, men's jackets, though there are not very many customers. There is a stack of freshly sawed lumber on the sidewalk, and two young men are carrying fifteen-foot boards through the crowds at considerable hazard to the heads of pedestrians, but the boys are adroit and lift and lower their burdens and wind their way along safely.

In the Piazza della Repùbblica the ravaged flower beds are heaped with new topsoil – one of the most cheering sites I have seen.

In Via Tornabuoni the shops are radiant with lights, and the polished show windows gleam with reflections from silver tureens, gold bracelets, and bronze statuary, from gold-banded Limoges china, from perfume bottles and jars of coloured bath salts. The two big book shops are open again, in the window of one of them a leather-bound French artwork, *Leonard de Vinci*, jostling the *Playboy Twelfth Anniversary Reader*, and a Pushkin lying next to Schlesinger's *A Thousand Days*. The street is as elegant as it once was, and tinsel and Christmas trimmings decorate the big showcases and the festive windows. There are pools of slime along the kerbs, but the sidewalks carry only a skim of dirt, nothing that we Florentines would call mud.

Nowhere, of course, is there any central heating, but small electric stoves in all the shops take the worst chill out of the air. The brilliant coffee shops on the corners are refurbished and reopened; in the big coffee shop under the arcade in Via Brunelleschi only one cashier is working and there is no heat, but the wide windows sparkle, the gold mosaics have all their old glitter, and the atmosphere is cordial.

Here at any hour of the morning you will find a crowd of men in gloves and overcoats, Florentine merchants again dressed with all their traditional polish, stopped in to warm the inner man with a good hot *espresso* and to enjoy a few minutes of lively talk – with gestures as fluid and expressive as a pantomimist's. You could not call the talk optimistic, though it is vigorous.

The debts incurred for beginning again are cripplingly heavy and customers are few, and there are lines and the grey colour of strain in the smiling faces. 'Perhaps by Christmas,' the men say, 'possibly by Easter'; and they give a wise shrug or a lift of their mobile eye-brows. '*Auguri*', they call as they go out of the doors; '*Pazienza*'.

On the way home I wind through torn-up streets where new water mains are going in. This reconstruction and the everywhere present earth-moving machinery are making it extraordinarily difficult for cars to get around, but there is a strangely gentler pace in Florentine traffic now, not the old screeching, dodging recklessness. Everyone seems to have learned a new gentleness.

CHAPTER SIX
Natale

Thursday, December 22

Today all the museums of Florence opened their doors to the public, a pre-Christmas treat for the city which has been promised for some time but hardly hoped for. They won't all be able to stay open, alas, but the beautiful art of the city is again on display. I climb the long stairs of the Uffizi (the elevators are out of order and sit for a long time in front of the Simone Martini 'Annunciation,' the Piero della Francescas, and the beautiful Masaccio 'Virgin with Child and Saint Anne'.

In spite of the mayor's confident promises that the town might be cleaned by Christmas, the task has proved far too great, and many streets are heavily encumbered, especially in the Santa Croce district and Gavinana above it across the Arno, where the army is still digging out and walls are toppling. The centre and the western Lungarno look bright and new, however, and Christmas shoppers throng the streets in a happy rebirth of trade. In the Movimento Forestieri, the offices on Via Vecchietti where tourists go to buy concert tickets and make railway reservations, the leaf calendar on the wall just above the streak of flood line stand in red at November 4.

This evening three American girls come to visit me, leaving their high, muddy boots outside the door in the entryway and treading in stocking feet across the marble floors to my room. I lend them slippers and shoes, and we make a pot of *espresso* and put Beethoven's Fourth Piano Concerto on the record player. They are tired and relax with contented sighs on chairs and rug. All three of them have been working for the past weeks, cleaning the marbles in Santa Croce. A distinguished English art restorer from the Victoria and Albert Museum, Mr. Hempel, is directing the efforts to save the tomb statuary and the other marbles in the church, using solvents followed by an application of talcum powder to get the *nafta* out of the stone. Fiery little Di, who is always angry and discontented, complains that the methods don't work; some of the oil stains are so deep that the solvents won't touch them and have to be applied over and over again.

'Nobody knows anything,' she says bitterly. Clare and Deborah, who are more temperate, protest that nobody can know anything, there aren't any precedents for this sort of salvage work. Never before in all history have marbles and paintings been sunk in mud and crude petroleum.

'Everything they try has to be an experiment,' they insist, 'and baffling as it is, a lot of it is coming off?'

'It takes so long. We aren't getting anywhere!' Di is feverish with fatigue.

'I know she's always fuming,' Deb tells me privately, 'but she makes up for it by working three times as hard as any of the rest of us. I love her.' Di is going to England for Christmas, where she will be put to bed for two weeks, suffering from exhaustion.

(I learn in February, after I have seen the restored and gleaming white marbles in Santa Croce, that the use of solvents followed by talcum succeeded in drawing the deep-seated *nafta* out of the stone but that some of the worst spots had to be done thirty times before they came clean.)

Clare tells us that she was at the Accademia two weeks ago, where the wet floor was buckling so badly that the 'David' of Michelangelo was tilting on its pedestal. Clare must return tomorrow to America, to complete her degree, and she is bitterly reluctant to leave. 'Let me know everything that happens in Florence – everything!' she begs us. 'I can't bear to go.'

They are completely unaware of doing anything extraordinary, these amazing young mud angels. Their response to the disaster was a spontaneous and common impulse, which has unified them in a way that sets them apart from the rest of us. Florence is their world now, and they bring her their love and themselves quite unselfconsciously and with frank gratification that the twentieth century has offered them something after all. All the adult rescue workers have tales to tell of them. On that first shocking dawn in Borgo Ognissanti, at the Hospital of San Giovanni di Dio, where the ground floor with its radiology laboratories went wholly under flood and *fango*, two hundred of them turned up in a body and set straight to work cleaning out, at a speed and with a thoroughness that no hired helpers, if such might have been found, could have equalled. One of the doctors, who was supervising there, told of seeing the son of a prostitute and the daughter of a duchess working side by side, 'cleaning out the johns'.

One long-haired beatnik boy, who had run away from home and had been tramping through the Balkans before he heard of the misery in Florence, told the same doctor that he liked the work in the mud. 'It's the first time in my life I've done anything for somebody else,' he said. Students from Milan are making a three-hour train trip every Friday as soon as school finishes, to pitch in here at hard labour, whatever is hardest, whatever is dirtiest; then they ride back on Sunday night to meet their Monday classes. Now that the long vacations are beginning, young people from all over Europe are giving up their holidays and are streaming into Florence to join in on the jobs. Caked with mud, both boys and girls, they are mucking out cellars, cleaning buildings, going down into blocked sewers to remove obstructions, doing whatever waits to be done – and so much waits to be done! The city government, in gratitude and to preserve their memory, is proposing to name a square for its *angeli del fango*.

Saturday, December 24

Christmas Eve, and the old towers of the city loom misty under frosty moonlight. The streets, which have been festive with throngs of Christmas shoppers these past days, are quiet and nearly empty, for the Pope is arriving in Florence to celebrate midnight mass at the great Duomo, and most of the citizens are already packed together in expectant crowds in Piazza San Giovanni before the cathedral.

I meet Deborah and we walk along the echoing waterfront under the moon. Evergreens and holly decorate the shop fronts, and even the places near the Ponte Vecchio which stand open and unclean are tinselled with some kind of Christmas trimmings. A vacant and littered opening that used to be a restaurant and now is only two walls has put out cedar branches and a big red hand-lettered poster: BUON NATALE A TUTTO IL MONDO. 'Look at that!' says Deb. 'Aren't these people wonderful?'

We are going to watch the arrival of the procession at Santa Croce, for *il Papa* will drive through the worst of the devastated districts as he comes into town, and the crowds should be thinner at Santa Croce than at the cathedral. We leave the broken waterfront and turn inland at the bridge.

In the Piazza della Signoria the ancient oil pots are alight on the Palazzo Vecchio, as they have been lighted yearly over the long centuries on Christmas Eve. The massive old palace, built like a fortress and battlemented, wears on its façade the red lily of Florence on a white shield, as well as emblems of the Guelphs and the Medici. It was erected in 1298 to house the city magistrates, and through republican and grand-ducal years, through the Risorgimento and the twentieth century, it has been the unchanging seat of Florentine government. Tonight above the vacant square, in every embrasure and window high on its stone front, in every crenel of the battlements and on each level of the tall square tower, the old palace glows with wavering small flames. Where the bell-tower rises against the remote sky under the moon, the flames of the oil pots flicker in the wind, a smoky dance of small fires that is lovelier and more ancient than any lighted Christmas tree. We stop short and look up at the old stones. We might be standing in the fourteenth century in this silent square on the night before *Natale*.

There is a big enough crowd before Santa Croce, though the middle of the square is clear, and there two young men with cameras are trying to clamber up the pedestal of the austere statue of Dante for a better look over the heads. We easily find a place in the third rank of watchers at the corner where the cars will enter, and we look around at the buildings, still darkly discoloured, the oil stains spread half-way up their second stories. People are sitting in the windows above us, but some of the shored-up houses nearby are dark and untenanted because of the peril of cracking walls and sagging floors. There has been little recovery around Santa Croce, and these squalid house fronts, their windows open for a night of celebration, hide a hundred stories of bravery or despair, of people getting along on next to nothing, or of the trifling loss, the one small blow too many, the ludicrously little thing that can bring on the end of the world.

I remember the couple in their sixties who were *alluvionati* and have been relocated near Santa Croce, and whose business had been the renting out of theatrical costumes and evening wear for formal functions. They were completely wiped out; all that was left them was two *frac* (tailcoats) and a costume for Father Christmas. In early December they were living in a cold fourth-floor room, where they had two straight chairs and some boards stretched on saw horses to serve as an ironing board. The two *frac* were usable and rentable and could be pressed, but the red costume was drenched and its white fur soggy. The wife was chattering like a squawking hen. The old man was ill and crying, actually crying, because his last hope had failed him: Christmas was coming close and here was *Babbo Natale* with his fur *inzuppata*. The strong-faced Italian noblewoman who is in charge of relief in this sector for the Anglo-American Committee and who introduced me to this couple told me that this was the only time since the disaster that she had seen a man cry. 'I myself never cry – in public,' she said to me, 'but to see a man so reduced, to see a proud man weeping – there were two small tears on my own cheeks. I could not refrain.'

I remember, more happily, the artisan in leather who has his workroom in his house and who lost all his leather and tools. He is a man in his thirties, living with his soft-spoken wife and twelve-year-old son in the dark rooms where they were flooded. Because he had been too poor to keep up his dues to the guild, he had not received any guild funds handed out just after the disaster, but he had gone right ahead and cleaned the house and had tried to repaint the walls, unsuccessfully, because the mildew came straight through. In the week before Christmas the couple had set up a very simple crèche in the entryway. The quiet, small-boned wife first started to apologize for the crèche – it was *umile* she was afraid; then she brightened and said, 'But I don't think *Cristo* would mind; he was born in a stall.'

A burst of clapping around us turns our heads toward the near street, young fathers lift small children to their shoulders, and two motorcycle policemen swing around the corner. They are applauded all the way up to the great church. Then with more police preceding it, the cavalcade appears, and the crowd cranes to peer into every car. Now the clapping really swells, and an open car slowly rounds the corner with the Pontiff, Paul VI, standing erect in white and crimson robes and wearing the white papal skullcap. He is a lean man with a distinguished and intelligent face. He keeps his arms raised and blesses the people as the car goes slowly by, and now we all move toward the steps of the church, which are blazing with floodlights.

The Pope is formally greeted by the Mayor of Florence; then he stands before the microphone and makes a brief speech to the assembled people, who are standing on tip-toe and stretching their necks, a couple of determined girls trying to push and elbow their way through to the front. The walls of the buildings around the square are so high and the loudspeakers echo so clamorously that most of his words are lost in the reverberations, but the loudest applause, without any question, is for his praise of the spirit of the Florentines and of the proud city on the Arno.

The floodlights glare, the cavalcade departs by the other side of the square, and most of the crowd follows. We turn back toward the sparkling tower of the Palazzo Vecchio and stroll home through the chill and lovely night along the deserted Lungarno beside a placid moonlit river, meeting only the indulgent interest of the *carabinieri*, who patrol in pairs.

Friday, January 6, Befana

The children of Italy do not receive their presents on Christmas Day, but on Twelfth-night, the festival of Epiphany, the coming of the Magi with gifts to the stable at Bethlehem. Epiphany is *Befana* in Italian, and *la Befana* is also the name of the benevolent witch of the holy day, who brings sweets and gifts to good children but who leaves a sock stuffed with coal for bad boys and girls.

This morning in the middle of the Ponte Vecchio near that statue of Cellini, where there are no shops and where the arch stands open above the water, there appeared hanging high a sock as big as the body of a man, chock full of coal, and bearing the legend: AL FIUME ARNO – *la Befana*'s present to the river.

CHAPTER SEVEN

Speriamo

Tuesday, January 31

All the month long the city has been coming back to its former shine, artisans starting to work again, the centre aglow, more shops opening, the pulse of the great town beginning to beat. Two weeks of severe cold in January fringed the borders of the Arno with ice, but now the weather is mild and in street after street basement windows are flung wide to dry out. One or two of the big hotels are open, but most of them are noisy only with the sounds of carpenters and plasterers and plumbers at their labours – and hotels account for only a small fraction of the rebuilding of Florence. All up and down the streets, in every block the air quivers to the tattoo of hammers.

At our small palace the old heating plant was dragged out in rusty chunks and fragments, and a new furnace has been installed, just in time to check the bands of mould that were forming along the base-boards and climbing up the walls.

Our Signora looks peaked and white after a succession of colds and influenza. The house is no longer nearly empty, our old friends the Consul-General and his wife having returned over a month ago, in time for Christmas and Dario's pate and turkey with chestnut stuffing; and a few tourists are starting to come in, some of them eager for the sight of horrors and rather disappointed to see the centre looking so handsome.

If you could not see beneath the surface, you would think the city to be on her feet again, but there are tell-tale signs if you know where to look for them. The long after-effects of the terrible drenching the city endured are just beginning to show up. Florence is wet, in some sections soaking wet. Dampness in the dwellings and *muffa* (mould) are doing damage now; in humid rooms in the unheated buildings the saturated walls are growing spots of fur or black blotches of mildew, and there is no way of drying out walls when the drenched ground under them sends of a steady infiltration of moisture. Three underground streams run beneath the city, one curving below the already *bagnata* Santa Croce area, and this doesn't help matters.

Although the ground floor of this house was not flooded, two weeks ago the parquet in my room began to erupt in little hills and fall apart. The underlying wet had so warped the hard oak that the separate strips of wood were curling into boat shapes – '*Il legno s'imbarca*,' the Signora said – and their cement base was water swollen and breaking up. I have been moved to another room overlooking the river, while workmen come in intermittently to tear out the old floor. And this is in a house where the heating has been restored.

A friend who has a second-floor apartment in the centre just now telephoned me to announce that her kitchen wall has suddenly become pregnant – a full pouch of plaster sagging out into the room overnight, as the water rising in the walls has caused them to settle and the plaster to soften. Downstairs a spring of water has begun to flow in the entrance, creating a constant pool through which the tenants must step on their way in and out, and hers is by no means the only building in which spring water is coming up through marble floors. 'Summer will get here eventually, and that should dry us out,' she says. '*Speriamo!*' Let's hope!

The economic life, too, is very shaky just now, though this insecurity doesn't show on the surface. Florentines are perfectionists, and their reopened shops are spotless and the displays are luxurious; yet even in the best shops there aren't a great many articles to choose from, and those shops that have some goods surviving from November are fortunate, indeed. A smudge of brown on a box of cosmetics or on the plastic envelope that holds a blouse or sweater means 'flood days'. Slowly the stocks are increasing as the artisans start to produce.

The serious problem now for the shop owners is debt. Except for the large enterprises with branches in Rome or Milan and an established American market, these small merchants were most of them in debt for the stock on their shelves when the *alluvione* struck them; the things they lost were not paid for, and those old debts hang heavy over them. Now there have been staggering costs for repair and rebuilding they have had to borrow heavily to buy new merchandise with which to start up again, and there have been long idle months with no trade, except for the brief flare at Christmas, while the interest on all these loans continues inexorably to mount. There are relief provisions for the postponement of interest, but this means a doubling of interest payments at the end of a year, a worrying prospect in these days while things stand still. When I go into a shop (the shop people can always spot an American), they ask me anxiously, 'Will they come back? Do you think the tourists will come back?' Then they give me their slow Florentine smile and spread out their palms in a brief gesture of irony, and add, 'Perhaps by Easter? Surely by summer? *Ebbene, speriamo!*'

'Our superficial wounds have healed but the deep wounds remain,' Mayor Bargellini said recently, and you need only step into the worst sectors to realize it. Conditions around Santa Croce are really shocking. In mid-January a thousand basements are still full of mud, and that mud has hardened so that soldiers and students digging out find their shovels bending, while buckets crack wide or are flattened by the solid weight thrown into them.

Many buildings near Santa Croce stand vacant, and few shops are open except for groceries, fruit stalls, and small coffee shops, where talk goes on. Streets are torn up, and there is no walking here without boots. Here too, all non-essential trades languish; only the lean necessities of every day are being bought. I visited a poor watch-maker, who has been furnished with tools by the guild but who has no customers. 'Who can pay for repairs? Who will buy watches now?' he asked with a grimace of resignation. He has paid what to him was a heavy price to restock the shop, the clocks and watches that had been left with him for mending at the time of the flood will have to be replaced, and he has no business. His wrinkled face was drawn with worry as he showed me two Topolino (Mickey Mouse) clocks – cheap wares sell best in this district – faces dented and works sprouting wires and springs. He stood shaking his head over them with a sort of wistful fatalism, and he did not want to talk.

Hardest hit of all the shop people are the antiquaries, through whose streets the Arno broke like a millrace and who were completely wiped out. Many of the treasures they lost were enormously valuable, among them medieval paintings and wood carvings that are irreplaceable, as well as porcelains and furniture from historic periods, old maps and icons. Generations of investments disappeared overnight and cannot be found again. Many of these dealers have rebuilt and have travelled to find new stocks to partly replace the old, at an appalling cost. Now they wait, and no one comes to buy. There will be buyers later in the year – they hope.

But the tone of life around Santa Croce is not so grim as all this sounds. I cannot forget the porter in one of the fine old palaces there who last week was showing me the water line around the courtyard – sixteen feet high and far above the arches – and was pointing out to me the great blotches of wet on the higher walls where water was seeping up above the second story.

'Wet, wet, everything is wet,' he said with an amused shrug, 'but summer will be hot, and then we'll dry out, we hope.' And at that point his lean ironic face suddenly broke into almost ecstatic laughter. 'We are full of hope, we Florentines,' he burst out, '*siamo vivi!*' – we are alive! and he flung out his arms as if to embrace the world. It is this delight in simply being alive in the good world that rings through the chorus of hope that we hear constantly now in the weakened but reviving town, Italians are realists and entertain no great dreams of future prosperity. The Florentines have gone through a full share of suffering in this generation: the war, the German occupation of the city, the bombardments, the German demolition of the bridges, the near starvation at the war's end, and the dragging years of poverty that followed. But if they have had to endure, they have lightened that endurance by a genuine delight in the small gifts that life is constantly showering on them. When they say, '*Speriamo*', the word is not tinged with resignation but really means, 'We hope'. We hope for a little safety and a few lire in the pocket again, we hope for the good sharp taste of a glass of Chianti and the crusty bread to eat with it, we hope for the summer sun to warm the towers and deep streets of our city, we want to take long walks beside the green river and drink in the refreshed beauty of our *cara Firenze* and see the colours of June on the hills, we hope to see our *bei bambini* (and they are adored by their parents, these pretty Florentine children) fat and well dressed and laughing. These are the good small gifts of life, and Florentines do not waste them or fail to relish them. *Siamo vivi!*

Tuesday, February 21

Spring is in the air, and everything waits in the state of mild tension, a tingling suspension that promises rebirth among the great stone streets at the same time that the grass turns bright with new green and the trees put out small leaves. There are signs of renewal among the great frescoes in the churches and the sculpture, the paintings that were drowned or damaged and whose survival is still being fought for. Only one per cent of the enormous heritage of art that Florence cherishes suffered injury on that cruel day in November, but that one per cent includes priceless works of genius.

The blank spaces on Ghiberti's lovely 'doors of Paradise' on the Baptistery still stand bare, but the magnificent panels are *in restauro*; there was some damage but it can be repaired, the chief problem now is cleaning them. The day is not far off when the morning sun will pick out in gold the craggy landscape where Abel dies at his brother's hand and old Adam drives an ox to plough the soil, and the same light will touch the perfect architectural reliefs and the grouped figures on the panels where Jacob is blessed by his blind father and where Joseph and his brothers in Egypt find the cup in Benjamin's sack. The south door of the Baptistery, which Andrea Pisano cast in bronze in 1336, is more seriously damaged, and nobody knows how to handle it.

I have been making a number of pilgrimages, in an attempt to take the temperature, if that doesn't sound too fanciful, of the convalescent city, to discover what is happening now to her libraries, her great art, and her people. Last week I paid another visit to the National Library on the upper Arno, a big vacant building these days, for the most precious volumes have long since gone to Santa Croce for restoration by experts, and the rest, except for some hundreds drying in the lower furnace areas, are up on the hilltop at Forte Belvedere. From hundreds of thousands of irreplaceable volumes the enveloping mud has been scraped off, patient hands have separated the pages and inserted thin sheets of paper (after a first abortive experiment with talcum powder served only to gum the pages together), the priceless books have been sterilized to keep mould from literally eating up the paper, and now they dry out and wait their turn for skilled care.

In one small area in the echoing space of the ground floor of the great library, half a dozen patient volunteers are bent over a long table, carefully scraping dried mud from the cards of the library catalogue, for only one layer of drawers of all the card files remained above water, and the cards were found scattered and mud matted all over the floors. Day after day big boxes of them go into the drying furnaces, and then one by one the cards are gently scraped clean by hand – those that are still legible, that is.

One of the volunteers is a merry little Englishwoman who came down to Florence at her own expense and who has been stretching the limited funds she was allowed to take out of England, in order to stay here and help in the rescue work a little longer. Now Italian friends have offered her a bed to sleep in, and she rejoices to have a few more days to spend at her modest and unexciting chore, scraping.

The vast areas of the underground stacks are hollow and damp and odorous, windows and doors wide open and furnaces roaring in some rooms. Archives, wrapped in paper, wait their turn in the dryers; and spread out on shelves in the drying rooms, ancient volumes lie open like fans, their dates reading 1581, 1600, 1612, 1632, 1692. The residue of mud was two feet deep down here, and there are still traces in corners and around door frames: here and there the floors are littered with file cards and detached pages. The walls leading down are elaborately decorated with patterns of hands, large and small, masculine and feminine, in brown impromptu designs where the students stamped their prints in *fango* for a memorial along the stairs where they formed their rescue lines.

In this vast underground five kilometres of stacks holding a million and a half books, mostly antique, went wholly underwater. Some books were glued to the ceilings by mud. All the bindings were ruined, for ancient leather does not take wetting, and there are dozens of refuse cartons of this old leather in hard lumps and strips, mixed with books that simply dissolved and were reduced to papier-mâché.

The Committee to Rescue Italian Art is committed to saving three hundred thousand rare volumes from this library and has already bought a book-binding machine – one book-binding machine a hopeful step but a very small one. 'In all Europe', says Professor Shell, director of the CRIA rescue work in Florence, 'there aren't enough binderies to rebind these books in our lifetime. It will have to be a great international effort.'

*

To enter the huge Church of Santa Croce nowadays is to walk into cleanliness and beauty again, for the floors are bright and the walls and statuary tombs white as of old; in fact, things are cleaner below the flood line. 'You don't really mean,' three American tourists ask me incredulously, 'that the water was in here this high?' But the evidence is written plain before their eyes. The intarsias are swathed in gauze waiting for rescue, and on the wet lower areas of the paintings along the aisles, the students have laid layers of rice paper to preserve the paint. Beside the choir in the Bardi and Peruzzi chapels, below the eloquent scenes from the lives of Saint Francis and Saint John the Evangelist frescoed by Giotto, fantastic heating devices brought in by CRIA from Germany direct their fires against the lower walls to dry them out and prevent the destructive upward seepage of water with its burden of paint-destroying salts. Three of the same sort of monsters are blazing away in the right transept below the frescoes of Agnolo and Taddei Gaddi. These big flame-shooting apparatuses look like red over-size cannons laced with woven wire, their mouths trained against the base of the walls below the endangered frescoes, their interiors a blazing fountain of rose and blue flares directed against the deadly areas of moisture. In the gloomy interior of Ognissanti at night they look more like engines of hell than engines of rescue, the fires roaring, flames streaking bright red in the dark like bundles of fiery spears in a net; but above them their light picks out all the pink and yellow tones in the frescoes and haloes them in rosy illumination, so that the saints in their soft robes appear to be blessing the infernal fires down below them.

All over town walls begin to glow clean and statues turn bright. And week by week the paintings that were lifted out of dark water and *fango* and carried to the Boboli Gardens behind the Pitti Palace for a first cautious cleaning are reappearing in refurbished beauty. Every few days completely restored panel paintings on wood are going on display in the long upper corridors of the Uffizi, and I make trips to welcome new ones, the marvellous old surfaces with their colours of red and blue and gold as smooth and the figures as harmonious and as haunting as ever.

Today, a grey spring day with a threat of rain, at the handsome Berenson villa, I Tatti, in the rolling hills of Settignano, Professor Curtis Shell, professor of art history at Wellesley and head of the Florentine Committee of CRIA, tells me about the enormous labours that have gone toward saving the endangered art of Florence: the wild confusion of the first week, when I Tatti was the one island above the city with both light and water; the rush of the students to rescue films, books, and paintings – 'Marvellous, the students have been simply marvellous!'; the speed with which the Committee to Rescue Italian Art sprang to life in the States, so that by the end of the first week the

Florentine contingent* was set up and functioning; the crash programme to save the frescoes; the struggle to rescue statues, wood-carvings, and tapestries; the architectural project – 'a hideously expensive item'; the patient restoration of books and paintings.

The professor is a soft-voiced man of sensitive face and faintly mocking eyes, who must be highly *simpatico* to the Florentines. Intensity burns in him, and his love for the works of art he is fighting to save turns his voice tender and his eyes bright when he speaks of them.

There is great hope for the frescoes, now that they are drying out, but even at this date it is hope rather than surety. The Giottos in Santa Croce are doing well, but there is worry about the Taddeo Gaddis, which contain some of the first examples of still life in Western art. In the Chiostro Verde at Santa Maria Novella, the Uccellos, which had the worst *nafta* bath, were already detached frescoes and are 'responding well'. There is worse damage in the Spanish Chapel, where the frescoes are part of the wall. The Botticelli and Ghirlandaio saints in Ognissanti have been cleaned (about twenty per cent of the surface of the frescoes was injured); 'it is a question of drying out and hoping'. Since these too are detached frescoes, there is more hope.

---

* Professor Shell's associates were Professor Juergen Schulz of the University of California at Berkeley and Dr. Eve Borsook, artist and internationally famed expert on frescoes, who lived in Florence for many years. Professor Millard Miess of the Institute for Advanced Studies at Princeton was chairman of the advisory board which dispensed funds.

At Santissima Annunziata, where the flood lay like a lake for days, the Castagno 'Trinity' is very fragile at the moment – 'it is touch and go'. And in the San Luca Chapel in the cloisters at the rear of the church there is seepage above the flood line on frescoes of Bronzino, Vasari, Pontormo, and Santi di Tito.

Restorers are still coming in, English, Dutch, and American; and German musical restorers are on the way. These skilled men will train Italian experts in the restoration of wood, textiles, and sculpture, for which arts, curiously enough, Florence has no staff; and CRIA is setting up a centre for the minor arts, to be headed eventually by a Florentine, where already such treasures as Donatello's 'Magdalen' and a little sixteenth-century hand-pumped pipe organ – 'an adorable thing' – are under care.

The wooden model of the Duomo made by Brunelleschi himself, which was torn to pieces by the flood waters, will be eighty per cent made whole again. In a work area covering huge floor spaces in the Pitti, the thousands of little pieces of wood are laid out, most of them still unidentified, but the reconstruction slowly progresses.

All the paintings from the churches and from the Uffizi storage rooms were transferred, after a first hasty cleaning, to the Limonaia, the huge greenhouses on the hill above the Pitti, where the paintings are being dried, and much faster than was first hoped. For the first restorations a mixed selection from the thirteenth to the seventeenth centuries has been chosen, and the timetable for the rescue of paintings is now three years, not twenty years or more as was forecast in the first dreadful days of ruin when hope seemed so thin. Old panel paintings on wood are the most endangered and will get first treatment; thin rice paper laid over the surfaces attaches and lifts up the paint while the old wood under it shrinks.

'There are some that will not be able to be saved,' Professor Shell says unhappily. 'There is terrible warping in the wood, and the colours are simply popping off.'

CRIA has just allotted two hundred and seventy-five thousand dollars for this restoration under the direction of Professor Procacci, Florentine Superintendent of Galleries. Funds are still coming in, but Professor Shell says with an expressive and almost Italian gesture of his hands, 'To be honest, nothing is enough!' The first aim of CRIA in the States was to raise two and a half million dollars. 'I could spend that tomorrow,' the professor says with realistic zeal. 'It may take thirty million.'

Still the whole picture is bright, and the man who bears so heavy a burden of responsibility for saving these menaced treasures of the ages is confident. 'We have great reason to hope,' he tells me, and I answer, 'It seems to me everybody in Florence is saying "*speriamo*" these days.' 'We say it too,' he says with a quick smile.

Friday, February 24

'The emergency period is over, but Florence is like a patient just coming out of a severe illness,' Mayor Bargellini says. '*È difficile ricominciare la vita.*'

And it is true that life is picking up again slowly and with difficulty. Most factory workers are back at their jobs, but Florence is not an industrial city. By far the greater part of her men are artisans. And while you may pass a woodworker's workrooms and see ornate picture frames being shaped at the lathes or a bookcase or chest of drawers in bright new lumber standing sanded and ready to be painted and touched up with gilding, this does not mean that these skilled men and their families or the families of the *operai* or the little shopkeepers are beginning from where they were in the easy prosperity of last October. They are beginning again from the very start. They have tools and a few materials, but their houses are empty of belongings and their pockets are empty of cash; they are only shakily on their feet and are living largely on debt and on hope and courage. These emotions can be read in the strong faces of the men, but many of their women cry at night.

Tears welled in the eyes of the wife of a small grocer in Borgo Ognissanti who, while she wrapped up my purchase of oranges, was telling me how they had managed to make a new start. Ceiling-high waters had gutted the shop and the back living quarters and had demolished their car. 'We had everything paid for,' she said; 'for the first time, after ten years, we were doing so well. Now not a thing is left. And everything costs more, we had to pay double to fill the shop again, and when there is no car to bring vegetables from the big market, what do you do? And how do we furnish the house? And now there are the children.' She was ashamed that I should see her sudden tears and turned her head away to dry her eyes and forced a quick smile. 'Better not to think about it,' she said firmly.

The greater part of the new city budget will go to enable labour and artisan production to move forward, the Mayor tells me this noon in his vast office, rich with medieval flavour, in the Palazzo Vecchio. 'We can no longer just spend to keep alive. We must re-establish these poor people.' It will not be easy; costs have risen, he says, but he believes the trades may recover completely within two years.

His Honour the Sindaco is a courtly gentleman with a distinguished old-Roman face, a coiner of aphorisms, '*Basta con il Cristo di Cimabue; ora bisogna pensare ai poveri Cristi*,' (Let's have done with the Christ of Cimabue; it's time now to think of the poor Christians), but a man with deep love for his city and its people, who is fighting against graver and more widespread troubles than any man could well contend with, a man who three and a half months ago faced a paralysed town, its centre a void, its vital activities extinguished, its gas lines and telephone and electric cables broken, its buildings gutted, streets torn apart, an incubus of mire, oil, and refuse to be dealt with, infection threatening, its people without water, hungry, shelterless, jobless, and cold, and its heritage of great art widely damaged. Florence has come unbelievably far since November. Mayor Bargellini thinks the city will be pretty well on its way by May. The Sindaco has been steadily optimistic since the disaster, and he has been sharply criticized for some of his too hopeful predictions, but this confidence of his has undoubtedly helped to keep up the people's courage during the black months of wearing patience and the need for patience.

Like the new city budget, Anglo-American relief funds are being spent now to re-establish small trades and thus lives. A sixty-year-old cobbler has been supplied with awls and leather; a milk shop has been furnished with jars and cans, a gift far better than money; a poor scholar has had his typewriter replaced. Dental machinery, woodworking tools, sewing machines for seamstresses, supplies for a hairdresser – these are the gifts that are turning the tide of life again in Florence. But the funds vanish too fast; there are too many of these small people in want. Generous waves of gifts from America and from England have preserved lives and are providing a first corner on security for many. With the British and American consulates acting together in a co-operative effort spontaneously generated immediately after the flood in response to the desperate need of the Florentine people, the Anglo-American Committee has worked entirely without overhead, its first headquarters set up at the British Consulate, its fifty to sixty volunteer field workers and thirty office workers putting in full days and months of unpaid labour.

Without a publicity campaign, depending only upon private letters of appeal, it has distributed £40,000 sent by the British people and $130,000 from Americans, all funds going directly to the relief of the destitute, and has helped to distribute nearly half a million dollars raised by Floreco, the American Relief Fund in New York. A further £155,000 from Britain has gone or will go toward art restoration through IAARF, Britain's Italian Art and Archives Rescue Fund. The Italian cities through their great newspapers have contributed substantial funds: from the *Corriere della Sera* of Milan a hundred and fifty million lire, all earmarked for art; from *La Stampa* of Turin a hundred and ninety million lire, an unrestricted gift.

'What will happen when the relief funds are gone?' I ask the Sindaco, and he says expansively that he hopes… And it is true that help for the destitute is still trickling in.

The sharpest need just now – and it has been the worst problem through all these hard months – is to find housing for the *alluvionati*. Hundreds of houses are gone in the flooded districts, and the number of dangerous dwellings increases daily as walls crack and ceilings fall. Many toppling houses are shored up and sealed, and the people who used to live in them are not even allowed to enter to find their belongings, because of the very real danger that the floors may collapse under them or the roof come down on their heads.

Even to bring the flooded families back to as many of their old homes as can be made liveable is not going to be easy. There must first be the long drying out, then repairs and cleaning, an assurance of sanitation; and there must be much caution to make sure the old buildings are safe.

The mayor wants a big building programme of cheap popular apartments with heat and decent facilities for the poor, to be paid for by the Italian state. The new subdivisions will have to go up in outlying areas, which are mostly low ground, and even at the most hopeful estimate it will take a year and a half to have them ready.

The ancient centre is sacrosanct and untouchable because of its beauty and its long history, but where it threatens complete decay, as in the Santa Croce district, something can be done to renew it. Santa Croce, one of the great sectors of ancient Florence, is now in many streets a slum. Some of these antique houses have only one toilet and one kitchen for all the families on all the floors, and many people now live there in dark rooms like caves in the stone, with narrow stone stairs curving damply upward from one decaying hall to the one above.

The Mayor has architects and engineers laying plans to revise and repair the interiors of the houses of this picturesque quarter, except for the ones that are hopelessly unstable and have no historic interest, for those will have to be torn down. Heat and modern plumbing and comforts will be provided inside the walls of the quaint old houses, but the outer walls, the narrow house fronts tucked in between palaces, the medieval lines, the uneven roof levels, the ancient cornices that almost meet overhead will keep the old flavour and aesthetic colour of vanished centuries. The Mayor in his enthusiasm for this Santa Croce project picks up a sheet of paper and a red pencil and begins sketching for me the lovely conformation of one of these thirteenth-century streets: it is the Florence of antiquity, and I can only be grateful that not only Florence but the whole nation of Italy jealousy guards its beautiful monuments of the past and that Italian law does not allow them to be destroyed or essentially altered. Once it is remade, the Santa Croce quarter will no longer be a home for the very poor.

There is renewal all over the city, but some of it is only temporary. The Lungarnos are solidly rebuilt, but the thin brick wall that again edges them is useful only to keep people on foot from stumbling over into the river, not to keep the river out of the streets. Pavements are being torn up for the replacing of broken water mains and old sewers, whose inadequacy and antiquity turned out to be a source of befoulment and a danger to health during the flood and the first bad weeks. New pipes are already being laid in a number of streets – to the dismay of the inhabitants there.

In Via dell'Anguillara and Via Nazionale the shop people are groaning and begging for relief, for their streets are deeply trenched, blocked, and stinking beyond belief as the old sewers come out, and it is somehow understandable that no customers are wandering down those streets ready to buy.

For a time the windows in Via Nazionale were hung with protest signs, but the signs disturbed the workers putting in the pipe lines and made them uncomfortable, so the shop people took them down. For the work has to be done. Most of the sewers of Florence were put in in 1851, which makes them ancient enough; and some of the oldest in the centre date from the time of Dante.

At the *Nazione* I check up on the charges of wrongdoing at the dams on the night before the flood. Four men are under criminal indictment for falsification of the records at the dams on that night, but for graver charges there is still only suspicion; the investigation is not yet complete.

Saturday, February 25

'This one we are coming to is a jerry-built apartment house, and the families who have been moved here come from some of the worst flood districts,' the worker from the Anglo-American Relief Committee tells me as the car winds through a narrow street called Via del Palazzo dei Diavoli. 'Where they come from, they have always lived looking over their neighbours' shoulders. Watch and see. No matter that I have to see only two of them; they'll all come out in the hall to listen.'

We are driving in Isolotto, an open and rather raw-looking housing development on the Arno downstream across Ponte della Vittoria, where many of the homeless families have been relocated. The car, its horn blaring at blind corners, twists past a few ramshackle houses and many three- or four-storey apartment units stuccoed in pale chrome colour and surrounded by blackened gardens, for the flood was here too, though not at its full force, and the shrubs and rosebushes look as if they had been painted with pitch: the *nafta* still adheres to them.

At the apartment house, a big-boned, dark, and good-looking young man comes running down the stairs to greet us with friendly and dignified courtesy. He is a taxi driver, my friend the worker has explained to me, an independent driver who owned his own cab, which the flood demolished; he has a wife and four-year-old son, and every article of their belongings was swept away. Now a full half of his income must go for payments on the new cab, and that leaves the family with just enough to pay rent and to eat on. They have a bed but no linens, a couple of chairs, a small table, a gas plate. The worker has been entrusted by the German Relief Committee with a gift of linens: four sheets, two pillowcases, three small bath towels, four dish towels, three hand towels, three table napkins; and these the young man receives with candid gratitude. He is assured and self-respecting, and he has no complaints, but speaks frankly and proudly of the way they are getting along. He taps his feet on the marble floor now and then to keep them warm; he is spotlessly dressed but wears no coat – he no longer possesses one. The worker has brought four men's jackets, and the young man tries one after the other, shrugging them off with a smile as they bind over his broad shoulders or as his big arms won't go into the sleeves; they are all too small.

Now on both sides of the hall, doors begin inching open, there is the sound of feet on the stairs, and shyly but avidly the neighbours slip out into the hall to watch and listen. Among them is a wizened young man with a face like a hopeful squirrel's, who wears a sheared-off cotton flannel bathrobe instead of a coat and is accompanied by a timid wife and a sturdy two-year-old boy.

'Who are you?' the worker asks, and the little man explains anxiously that they have just come down from Gavinana, where it was so wet and so dangerous that they didn't know whether they would live from one day to the next.

'Dear me, even after four months they keep popping up like this,' my friend exclaims to me, 'and I don't know what we are going to do. Our funds are gone, and I'm supposed to be finishing the work here, but these people need so much, and they are so understanding and patient they'd break your heart. I can't bear to come back here when there is nothing I can do for them.'

But our young taxi driver is excited: he is sure one of the small coats will fit this young man in the truncated bathrobe. So again we have a trying on, and the little man is persuaded to forgo the impressive but thin Palm Beach coat and to take a slightly worn but much warmer tweed jacket which will shield him against the winds of March. The young taxi driver is pleased and proud; he has adopted an almost paternal attitude toward his undersized neighbour. A child's sweater is found for the two-year-old boy.

Now a haggard young woman creeps down the stairs, wearing a thin wrapper over her dress for warmth, and she is the second 'case' my friend has come to see. In tense and agitated phrases she keeps saying she has no home to return to, her house has *crollata*. She describes excitedly how they had to break a hole in the roof to climb out above the tumbling waters, how out there clinging to the tiles her husband suddenly went out of his mind and began raving and was taken away by rubber boat to the mental hospital, how she is left alone now with an asthmatic child, without any resources, with nothing to live on. In her barren apartment there is only a crude bed and a rusty two-burner gas plate set up on bricks to lift it off the floor a few inches; there is no table. She too receives a gift of linens, and the worker promises with pained sincerity to do the very best she can to get some money for the wretched woman. Everybody shakes hands with us as we leave.

In a street of small antique houses, behind a thick wooden door with a highly polished brass knocker, we find an energetic young man, a silversmith who had his forge in his house and worked at home and who has just re-established himself. He leads us happily through small arched doorways and clean rooms with damp floors where there are a few pieces of reclaimed furniture. Everything in the old house went underwater, and the place oozes with wet. My friend has brought a gift of knives, forks, and spoons and occupies herself with the wife, but the young silversmith is interested only in showing me his forge and the pieces of silver he is working on. The ancient workroom is at the back of the house and is walled with brick, and we step across a puddle on the floor; a rough table, a small forge, and a few shelves have been set up again; there are two good windows to provide light. The young man is repairing silver candlesticks, all of the same pattern, and he holds one affectionately in his hands and turns it gently while he explains the process to me. The lines are good, the raised pattern around the base elaborately executed, the craftsmanship flawless; the young man's face is lively with an artisan's pride in his skill, and his fingers caress the silver. Fondly he replaces the candlestick on a shelf and brings out a small finished bowl. He finds it almost impossible to break away from the pleasures of his workshop when my friend comes back to tell me we must go, and she too has to be shown the new work and must ask questions about it. We return to the kitchen, where their three-year-old daughter is sitting on the table, wrapped in a blanket and feverish; it is the dampness in the house that has been too much for the child, who has caught a cold on her chest, the young mother explains. '*Troppo presto*,' the father agrees with a fatalistic smile. We came back too soon.

'You ought to see some of the farmlands to the west,' my friend says to me when we are in the car again. 'Very few people have any idea how far this privation and destruction stretches; there are endless miles out there where there is simply nothing left. And she tells me of a farmer in his sixties who with his seven children huddled on the farmhouse roof with the flood swirling at the eaves for nearly forty-eight hours until he finally attracted the attention of a helicopter by firing off his hunting rifle. 'Their cattle were all drowned, all they had left was a little wine, there was no food. When they could return home, the house was threatening to fall down, and the owner, who lived at Pisa, never came near.' Shortly before Christmas the Anglo-American committee reached the Family with a little food and a gift of fifty thousand lire which is about eighty-five dollars. 'I wish you could have seen him a big strong husky man who had never cried in his life,' she says with feeling, 'but he cried when he received the Christmas gifts.' Now one son has been able to get a job at two thousand lire a day, and the whole family is living on that. The farmer finally got enough to buy one cow – he had lost ten animals. There are thousands of families living like this now.

My friend the worker, after a distinguished career in the arts in America, came to live in Florence six years ago and has an easy command of Italian. She has been devoting all her time to relief work in these hard months.

'I cannot tell you how much I admire these people,' she says. 'They are extraordinary. In spite of all they have lost and all they are going through, they never complain.' Then she makes a wry face and qualifies the statement, and describes a slum district where the dwellers are wholly illiterate and have always been miserably poor. There, once they get the idea that money is coming from America, 'where everybody is a millionaire', the wretched folk clamour to be provided with a standard of living they have never known and can never hope to know, and they grow loud and indignant when this sudden dream fails them.

But among artisans and workmen there is courage, pride, and a cheerful patience that has carried them through catastrophe and will outlive hardships. And it is going to be hard for a long, long time.

Young married couples like those relocated in Isolotto cannot hope to re-establish the kind of modest comfort in which they began their married life, before the flood took away their homes. Most of them now have young children, and even though the husband may be working again, they are paying high rents here, and their old dwellings may never again be habitable. They cannot buy new furniture, stoves, bedding and linens, dishes, rugs, curtains – all the pleasant paraphernalia of family life that were swept away in a black night and a day of storming waters. The young wives grieve most of all for the loss of their big chests of linens, which Italian girls spend years buying, hemstitching, and embroidering and which are their chief contribution to the marriage.

At a solid stone and stucco apartment house we meet Pietro, a young mason with a head of curly light-brown hair and the big blue-grey eyes ringed with dark lashes that are a characteristic of the Tuscan people. He has an injured back and cannot work, yet he carries himself well and greets us with pleasant cordiality and innate dignity. Only a few streets away from the family's present quarters stands the little house where they used to live *sottosuolo* and where the flood caught them. Pietro is eager to show it to me. We go down six or eight steps below the sidewalk to the entrance and come into four good-sized rooms whose windows, high in the walls, are just at ground level. The house is completely empty, perfectly clean, and wringing wet, and the walls are streaked with mildew.

Pietro has a fine sense of drama, and he acts out for us with gestures and with considerable humour the arrival of the flood in the first grey hours of dawn on November 4. He and his wife were wakened by a great gushing and splashing in the bathroom: the drains were backing up and the toilet and basin were spouting water. The couple stumbled out of bed to investigate and found themselves in water to their knees, the flood already in the house. 'It was the bathroom that saved us,' Pietro says with a huge laugh. They caught up their seven-year-old son and fled through the swirling streets. Now they wait, who knows for how long, until things begin to dry out. On the days when his back allows him to work for a few hours, Pietro has covered the bathroom walls with new bright tiles, for the flood ripped the old tiling off the walls.

In the first month and a half Pietro and his family received twenty thousand lire (about £11) in relief money, and by now, over four months, the sum has been brought up to seventy thousand lire in all. '*Io sono molto contento*,' Pietro says with a smile of frank acknowledgement of his good luck, and he formally presents his small son, who shakes hands with us steadily but shyly, looking up at us through long lashes out of eyes of the same blue-grey as his father's.

In another well-built apartment house, this one with an elevator and central heating, we visit the family of a young typesetter, a lean blond boy in his early twenties, with a high forehead, classical features, and intelligent light grey eyes. His wife is short, dark, light-eyed, and girlish. The kitchen contains new furniture: a plastic-topped table, two tubular-framed chairs with plastic seats, and a highchair. There is a wooden table in the dining-room with two small piles of baby clothing and diapers folded upon it, nothing more. A two-year-old girl in a fresh blue pinafore peeks at us, poking out a curly topknot from behind a chair. A wail comes from the bedroom, and the wife brings in a fat baby in a fuzzy pink sleeper. The children are wearing brand-new clothes.

The young parents, however, are dressed in what are obviously ill-fitting relief garments. The young man shows off the thin grey sweater that serves him for a coat and explains that when it was given to him it was much too short and he himself knitted the long cuffs and waistband of black wool that have made it fit.

The flood took everything these two owned, and for twenty-four hours they were isolated by the waters and in great fear, for their baby was due to be born on the day of the flood itself and they were completely out of touch with the world. 'She is a very good *bimba*, the father says; 'she waited five days to be born.'

They have received no relief money. The young man is working, and because in their desperation they found an apartment for themselves instead of waiting for the city to place them, they did not receive the rent compensation that the city paid to displaced families for three months. Out of a monthly pay check of £57 10s. 0*d*., £27 5s. 0*d*. goes for rent. On top of this there are bills for heat, gas, light, and water; and there is the new furniture to be paid for, the children's clothes, transportation, milk, and food, which is expensive in Florence.

The young man wants urgently to know why the relief funds were not evenly awarded. He is not angry, he is not a troublemaker, he insists; he just wants to know, and he is independent and stubborn about it: it is not just their own case, he knows of other inequities. My friend takes him with complete seriousness. He should recall with a clear memory, she urges, just exactly what things were like in those first terrible weeks, with thousands upon thousands of families stripped and desperate for shelter and for food to put in their mouths. It was unparalleled confusion, and the best that could be done was to hand out aid swiftly to the worst of the *alluvionati* wherever they happened to appear. How could there help being inequities when everyone was driven by emergency and only time mattered?

She looks him in the eyes with knowing gravity and he meets her look with clear intelligence. 'This is not the right way to feel; you must be careful or you will build a grievance,' she says, and then adds firmly, 'You Italians are a highly gifted people, but you must understand yourselves. You have great gifts: you are sensitive, you are craftsmen, you have a fine talent for music, you are artists; but you have absolutely *no* gift for organization – none at all!'

The young man's square jaw relaxes, and the grey eyes acknowledge the justice of what she is saying and light up with reluctant amusement. '*Giusto*,' he says with a smile and a shrug. Then his face clears and he squares his shoulders 'I must say to you that I think we are *fortunatissimi*,' he says deliberately. 'For my wife and babies I have a clean apartment with heat,' and he is suddenly so overcome by his good fortune that he wants to offer us a glass of wine.

'Aren't they splendid types, these young people, like Pietro and this boy and the taxi driver?' my friend demands as we go on our way, after our young man has escorted us to the car, opened the doors for us, and shaken hands with the elaborate and warm good manners that distinguish these people. 'They are so clean cut and independent. They will do well for themselves.' She adds thoughtfully, 'These Florentines haven't suffered any spiritual damage from this flood, just the opposite.'

Saturday, March 4

It is four months today since the *diluvio*. The spring sky is deep blue, as only Italian skies can be blue, and the strong sunlight lays a dust of gold on the villas and olive groves on the hills. On the riverbank below the wall, the flattened black trees that lie on their sides along the sand and that we have all been sure were dead are sprouting new leaves and shimmer with frills of faint green. Young couples stroll along the Lungarno with their arms around each other's waists.

A man in his thirties is singing in full voice as he walks down the street. When I paid my first long visit to Florence, a good many years ago, one of the most agreeable recollections I took back with me was the sound of resonant male voices bursting into song along the streets at night; but in the intervening years with the predominance of radio noise and the importation of rock and roll, this pleasant custom disappeared from the Florence of the evening. Now, as I have become happily aware in these past weeks, hardly an evening passes without at least one song rising on the night air under my windows. Sometimes it is an aria, and in that case of course Verdi, since Italians are enamoured of Verdi; but usually it is an Italian love song, sighing, lamenting, desirous, and melodious: '*Colgo la rosa e lascio star la foglia; ho tanta voglia di far con te l'amor*', or '*Ritorn amore, mi troverai*', in strong bass or baritone. With the return of spring sunlight there is singing in the streets by day.

In the late afternoon I take the *cicolare* bus up through the hills to San Miniato, where there is a fine view of the city from above. All Italians are rude when they try to board a bus, crowding and elbowing and stepping on toes, and in this operation the Florentines are no exception; but once aboard they revert swiftly to their traditional courtesy. A big military-looking man comes on carrying a cane, and a young man who is taking his girl for a Saturday outing is on his feet in a flash to offer his seat. The military man insists on giving the seat to a woman, there is bowing and smiling, and everybody is pleased. At one stop a tiny white-haired grandmother crawls aboard, a fragile shell of an old woman in a swathing of black shawls; and the whole bus becomes alert. Half-way down the car a young man taps the shoulder of the youngest person who is seated, and she gets up at once, but the seat is far from the door, and every person in the intervening seats moves up one space. Two men take the little grandmother by her arms, and a woman at her back steadies her by the waist until she is safely deposited in the nearest chair to the door. The bus sways and climbs among villas and gardens, where plum trees are white with blossom above the walls. Tennis courts are crowded with jumping teenagers, and on a miniature roller-skating rink out in the air small children are wheeling unsteadily and bumping into each other.

At San Miniato, in front of the exquisite little church, the oldest in Florence and a gem of Romanesque architecture with its gold mosaic and its rounded arches, I find a bench in the sun and look down over the rosy tiled roofs of the city on the Arno. To my left the ancient fortress block of Forte Belvedere joins the battlemented city walls of a much earlier Florence, and below these dark walls olive trees are a cloud of whispering silver foliage. Among formal flat-topped pines, cypresses stand up like black slender candles against a sky that is turning pink with sunset. Above the wave of tiled roofs the white cathedral rises, its perfect rose-red dome floating like a great bell suspended over the city, and Giotto's delicate white *campanile* stands slender and safe at its side. The sturdy block of the Palazzo Vecchio with its square tower looms black against a flowering sky, for the sunset has begun to bloom red as a bowl of roses. The palace fronts along the Arno have turned orange in this warm light.

The town itself seems to be breaking into rosy flower in the spring sunset, and this is of course the meaning of its name, Fiorenza, the flowering town, the city of the red lilies that flame on its white banners. The lilies have recently been drowned, but like all hardy flowers with their roots in the muck, they are coming into undiscouraged bloom again. It seems a good omen, the sight of the flowery city under the red sky.

I think back to the days of the mud, the stench, the horror; the days of dogged and independent labour in cold, wet, and ruin. I remember the bright-faced students plastered with *fango*, the gallery people who struggled in hip-deep water to save the paintings. I think of the civilized grace of a people who could rejoice together over the rescue of a Botticelli while they declined to grieve over their own losses. I remember the grave courtesy and the curious gentleness and concern they displayed to one another and to those of us who remained among them, a graciousness that had almost been lost in the prosperous years but that now blooms again as the one necessary ingredient of recovered life. I think of the patient breadlines and the water queues, and of the woman who called to me, '*Bisogna cantare*'.

I remember the brave little sign APERTO – SI RICOMINCIA and the dry humour that began to exert itself above the desolation, the signs advertising MUD BATHS above the swamps in the streets. I recall the two young men with nothing left who said, '*Sono molto contento,*' 'We are *fortunatissimi*.' Deeply injured as Florence may be, I think, she is rich in her citizens, in their civilized dignity and in their choice of creativity and integrity as the two solid gifts of life to be saved when everything else had sunk out of sight – and in their unflagging courage. And it occurs to me that that first citizen of Florence, Dante, if he had seen the conduct of his people in these anguished months, would have forgiven them everything he ever blamed them for, would have felt his own demanding, proud, and fiercely loving spirit to be fulfilled in them. I believe he might award them an accolade he offered to a Fiorenza of an older day than his own

così bello viver di cittadini ... a così dolce ostello.*

---

* So fine a life of citizens ... in so sweet a dwelling place. *Paradiso* XV: 130, 132

CONTRIBUTORS

Kathrine Kressmann Taylor (1903–96) was born in Portland, Oregon. She studied English literature and journalism at the University of Oregon, before moving to San Francisco. In 1928, she married Elliott Taylor, an editor and owner of an advertising agency. During the Great Depression, the couple lived on a farm in Oregon before relocating to New York. After World War Two she became a lecturer, and then the first female tenured Professor at the University of Gettysburg, Pennsylvania, where she taught for nearly twenty years in the English department before retiring and making her home in Florence, Italy. In 1967, she was remarried to John Rood, a sculptor, dividing her time between Minneapolis, Minnesota and a villa near Florence.

Vanessa Nicolson is an art historian and journalist and is also the author of two memoirs, *Have You Been Good* and *The Truth Game*. Her novel *Angels of Mud* is set in 1940s London and 1960s Florence, and tells the story of the aftermath of the floods there. Vanessa spent her childhood in Florence, travelling between a British father and her Florentine mother and lived through the devastating events of 1966. She graduated from Sussex University in Art History and Italian in 1979, began her career at the Tate Gallery, and has since worked as a feature writer, reviewer, curator and film programmer as well as an interviewer for the British Library Sound Archive 'Artist's Lives' project, making recordings with artists such as Anthony Gormley.

Vanessa is married to the journalist and writer Andrew Davidson and lives in Sissinghurst, Kent.

Agnesbic is an Italian/British illustrator based in Sussex, UK. Her work draws inspiration from a love of mid-century design, travel, and the warm colours of Tuscany, where she grew up. With bold colour palettes, economic use of lines and closely observed details, Agnes's compositions are simple yet striking, distinctive in their characterful optimism, youth and elegance. Her designs have been commissioned by a wide range of international companies and institutions, including Harrods, the *New York Times*, Soho House, Simon & Schuster, Virgin, *NY Mag*, *Vanity Fair* France, Chronicle Books, Victoria's Secret, Bergdorf Goodman, UBS and *Elle* magazine, among many others.

agnesbic.com

MANDERLEY PRESS TITLES

***Edinburgh: Picturesque Notes* by Robert Louis Stevenson**
Introduced by Alexander McCall Smith
Illustrated by Iain McIntosh

***The Armourer's House* by Rosemary Sutcliff**
Introduced by Lara Maiklem
Illustrated by Isabel Greenberg

***Appointment with Venus* by Jerrard Tickell**
Introduced by Rosa Rankin-Gee
Illustrated by Edward Bawden

***The Fly on the Wheel* by Kathrine Cecil Thurston**
Introduced by Megan Nolan
Illustrated by Fatti Burke

***Letter from New York* by Helene Hanff**
Introduced by Jean Hanff Korelitz
Illustrated by Bruce Eric Kaplan

***China Court* by Rumer Godden**
Introduced by Linda Grant
Illustrated by Emily Maude

***The House in Cornwall* by Noel Streatfeild**
Introduced by Lucy Mangan
Illustrated by Elly Jahnz

***Tales of London Town* by Joan Aiken**
Introduced by Kiran Millwood Hargrave
Illustrated by Annabel Pearl

***Florence: Ordeal by Water* by Kathrine Kressmann Taylor**
Introduced by Vanessa Nicolson
Illustrated by Agnesbic

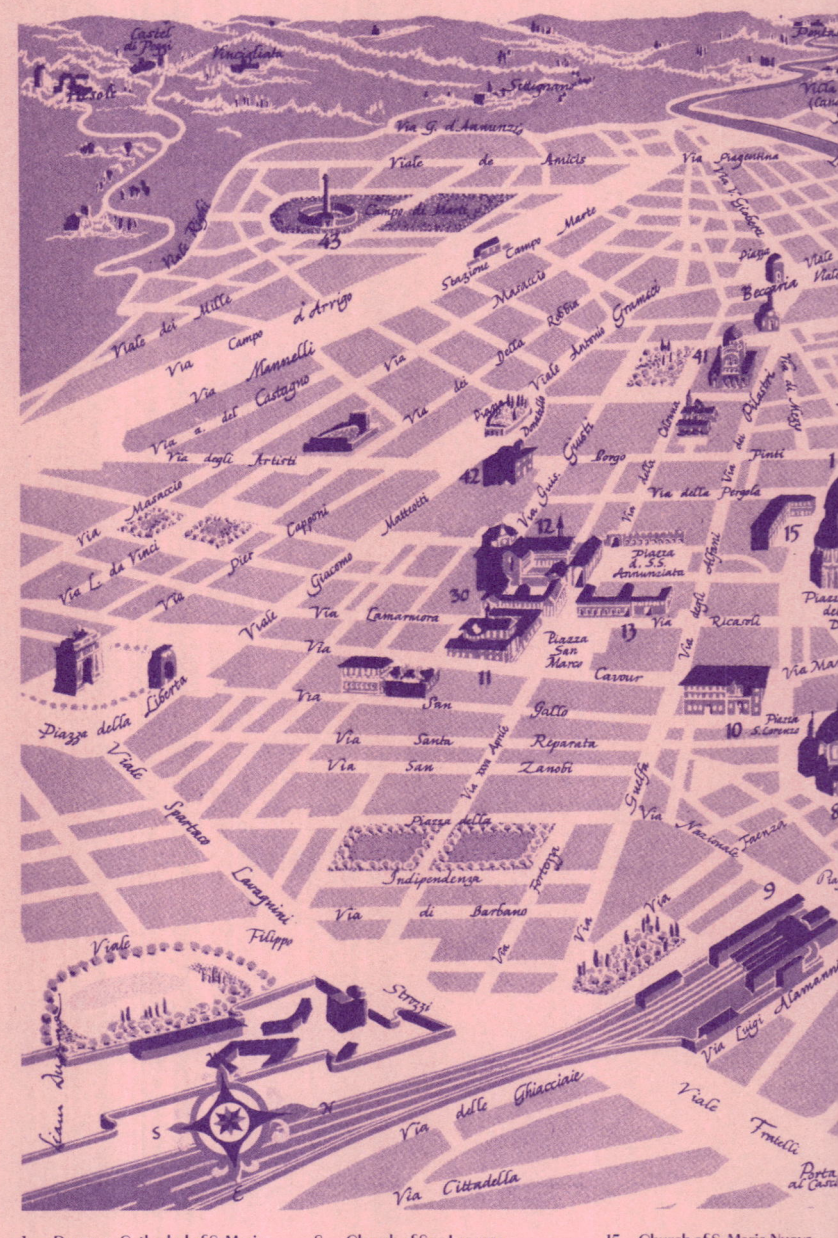

1 Duomo – Cathedral of S. Maria del Fiore	8 Church of San Lorenzo	15 Church of S. Maria Nuova
2 Baptistry of S. Giovanni	9 R. R. Station	16 Church of Orsanmichele
3 Palazzo Strozzi	10 Palazzo Medici-Riccardi	17 National Library
4 Palazzo Vecchio	11 Church of San Marco	18 Bargello (National Museum)
5 Uffizi Gallery	12 Church of the S. S. Annunziata	19 Church of S. Trinita
6 Church of S. Maria Novella	13 Galleria dell'Accademia (the Academy)	20 Opera House (Teatro Comunale)
7 Church of Ognissanti		21 Church of S. Maria del Carmine
	14 Pensione Consigli	22 Church of S. Spirito